FROM THE LOST LETTERS
SENT - BOOK TWO: 1992 - 1993

FROM THE LOST LETTERS SENT - BOOK TWO: 1992 - 1993

Memoirs From An Invisible Songwriter

LORD CHESTER L. BALDWIN II

A Lord Baldwin Happening

Contents

I

FROM THE LOST LETTERS SENT -

MEMOIRS OF AN INVISIBLE SONGWRITER

BOOK TWO: 1992 — 1993

2

AUTHOR'S NOTES

FROM THE LOST LETTERS SENT

Memoirs From An Invisible Songwriter
Book TWO: 1992 - 1993

What we have here is the second book (of four) that documents the lyrics and memoirs of the first 44 albums of Lord Baldwin, (Lord Chester L. Baldwin II).

Originally the title of these books was going to be, "Words For Songs," but one night I was lying in bed trying to go to sleep and thinking I needed something else; something that could signify the state of affairs that is Lord Baldwin's music and the songs he writings. In 1989-1990 I started recording songs that I had written words for, or music I had composed and kept in my head since 1966.

These 44 albums, categorized as the "Archive Series," were recorded during the, "Analog" era. The varied recordings were accomplished using a TASCAM 4-track Cassette Recorder. Book TWO, represents the recordings of the second nine albums of the Analog era;

10 – Heaven
11 - A Long Way From My Home
12 – You've Got To Believe
13 – A Family Man
14 – Another One Of Those Days
17 – Voices From The Past
18 – More Of The Same
19 – Expecting Rain
20 – Plastic On Plastic

When I created the first two albums and shared them with my family and friends, I was told that I should sell my cassettes to the music stores but I let them know that it was my hope and mission to create this portfolio of material, put music to the words, poems, lyrics, record the instruments, record my voice, engineer the production of the album, and then it is my mission to share that gift and talent with others. Yes, there always was that erstwhile element in the mix; the ego wants his genius to be known and compensated, but as that continued to never happen, to keep chasing the dream, there would have to be a different motivation. So, as I continued to give my work away, (since 1990), it was like a thank you to my Heavenly Father for the gifts and talents of music. But thinking spatially, I thought as how each one of my songs was kind of like a special letter, with its own individual message maybe making a statement before it is sent out there into the vastness of the universe, into space, a letter from me to you. At a unique and particular occasion, each letter (song), with their time postmarked on the outside, would go out into the universe, maybe contemplating their hopes that the message would be received sometime, maybe not today, maybe not tomorrow, but someday. And these lost letters sent have been drifting in time and space for years, waiting, hoping for someone to find and open them, and read (hear), its message. And these lost letters are out there right now in the incalculable vastness of the cyber-digital cosmos, waiting to be discovered, calling out, "Come find me."

In case you have decided to skip past Book ONE and go directly to, 'From The Lost Letters Sent - Book TWO, please note that the contents of all the books can be broken down into three parts;

First, **the Album Cover Art**, which, as noted previously, I'm delighted with, because I had such fun designing and creating them (as an icon if you will), to represent the songs, the music, the lyrics and poetry of that particular album.

Second, **the Words, the Lyrics, the Poetry** – These "Words For Songs" come to me in my daily doings, when I'm riding my bike, when I'm trying to go to sleep and sometimes they come to me in my dreams. Sometimes playing my guitar invites the words for songs to come out and play. Sometimes I take an interest in a happening that needed documentation, even if it is just lyrics to a song. Sometimes I am driven by the administering of injustice and inequity to the down-home folks that have to deal with prejudice and discrimination just to live a life here in America, and I am driven to write a poem to reflect the way I am feeling at that time. I believe in the potential of each song being important, in part from its individual contribution and to its possibilities as a whole especially if it is a concept album. For that sometime in the future.

Third, we have the, "**Memoirs From An Invisible Songwriter**" which in and of itself is broken down into two parts; **Part One**; a collection of stories that may, or may not relate to the writings of the words for songs, and, **Part Two**; the documentations of past happenings, to give life to and clarify particular happenings, shed light on projects, explaining where I was, and what was happening at that time in my life, and then perhaps why it was that I felt the need to write the words I did, explain the challenges, the triumphs and failures, and reasonings, and decisions to the song's creation.

As I was originally putting this document all together in 2001, as a project that I was doing at The Evergreen State College, some of the stories and antidotes, fresh at the time, made a lot of sense, so I included them. Besides being fun diversions to the whole, I believe the stories to be essential to help you gain a more balanced understanding, and it was my hope that some of the stories could shed light on who I was, what I was doing, my motivations and what it was that shaped me to go in the directions I did and why I did not go in other directions when the opportunities presented themselves.

Regrettably, there is always so much more to include, but I needed to keep moving to get this work out and so, what you have here is not complete, nor do I think it ever will be. It is a work in progress though, and I reserve the right to revise, renew, renovate and or bring the "**Memoirs**" and "**Stories**" up to date.

Accepting the fact that the twelve percent accomplishments come at the time spent and expense cost of the eighty-eight practice writings that would eventually become, "just not good enough." Still, inside those twelve percent pieces some masterpieces have manifested themselves.

As Lord Baldwin's music is now streaming worldwide, this book may act as a companion guide for the listener of Lord Baldwin's material, and for those who might be interested in what thought-processes and insights that Lord Baldwin was going through or was influenced by, along with stories that may be related to the creative processes.

PERHAPS SOME BACKGROUND

In the mid-50s, my family was living in Iron Mountain Michigan where I was influenced early on to what music was all about and listening to the birth of Rock and Roll in my older brother John's bedroom. After my brother David, John's favorite brother, left in 1958, I was delegated to try to fill the gap that David's departure left, and so, while John and I would sit on his bed playing a variety of card games, we would be listening to music on his Westinghouse Tube Radio. From fan magazines of that era, like; "**Teen**" and "**Hep Cats**" and "**Dig**" and "**Rock and Roll Songs**" (a few of the titles that John collected along with his "**MAD**" magazines), John was well read and seemed to know everything about the artists that we were listening to, and he loved to share that information, telling me narratives and stories about his favorites; Elvis Presley, Ricky Nelson, Chuck Berry, Bill Haley and the Comets, the Platters, Fats Domino, Gene Vincent, Little Richard, the Diamonds, Pat Boone, the Everly Brothers, the Coasters, Sam Cooke, Jerry Lee Lewis, Tommy Edwards, Conway Twitty, Connie Francis, Jackie Wilson and Buddy Holley. My love for the music only grew even after John went into the navy in 1960.

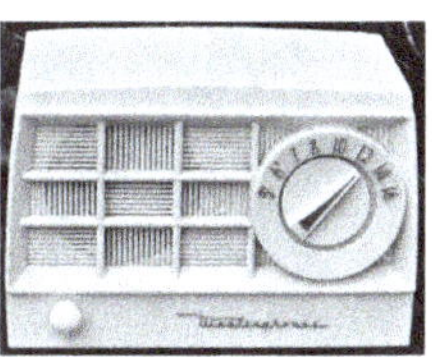

Sadly, maybe six months later, my mother grabbed us kids and ran away (for the second time) from her abusive husband, (we'll just call him; Senior). There was very little time to prepare for the departure and we would be traveling light by Greyhound bus with no space to take wanted possessions; only a change of clothes. I thought that we would be returning after their reconciliation, so I felt all my prized-good stuff was safe. And even years later, knowing the house on Margaret Street had been sold and others were now living there, I felt that I'd be able to go back to that house in Iron Mountain and go into that closet and retrieve all those treasures. That of course, never happened.

My 1963 Fender Acoustic King Guitar

Okay, okay, getting off track here. It is obvious that I don't know what to say here or how to say it. Maybe you're asking yourself, why should I care about this book? What is so special about it, and who is this self-proclaimed Lord Baldwin? Maybe this Author's Note might sound better if it was presented from the third-person perspective or point of view, kind of like an outsider looking in? Let's try that out and see.

TASCAM 4-track Cassette Recorder From The Lost Letters Sent

Many aspire to do great things, especially when they recognize that they've been entrusted with particular talents and gifts. It takes time and soul searching to discover the potential of those gifts but even from the beginning of the process, some begin to sculpture and to feed and to modify and to nurture their special dreams that they might grow into that distinct singular vision of that one day, where they will shine and be able to bask in their own bright starlight.

What happens when that dream that we have been working with for so long, continues to be three or four steps in front of us? What if we can even visualize the dream and see it in motion with others that are moving about, wearing that dream; our dream, meanwhile, that same dream for us continues to be beyond our reach? In spite of all the discouraging voices steeped in negativity, we have to choose to listen to our heart. We must continue to plod on; we are, after all, on a mission. Never mind the great ones out there on center stage. Never mind the critics that pan your work and criticize your ineptness. And never mind the time it takes to complete that one simple expression of words and music that, arguably pales in the light of the others. **We are on a mission**; a mission to find our words and our voice and our chord progressions and our vision of what we want others to know us by. We must continue to move forward. and in doing so, knowing that things too easily gained are too little esteemed, **we keep chasing that dream**, no matter how far in front of us it gets. We can't give up; we refuse to give up. We know that if we want this thing to work, **we've got to believe**.

As this book will probably be read on a computer monitor or through a phone, illuminating your display of the pages, it is good to know that the book also includes all of the ten album's cover art and in full colour representations. There are also liner notes about the covers included on the back pages of the album art itself, explaining some of the reasoning for Lord Baldwin's art designs; each an esoteric work of computer art and worthy of being displayed on good-quality, long-sleeve tee-shirts; you know, the ones with at least three or four buttons in front like the ones in head shops in 1968?

Lastly, (what does that really mean, lastly?). I want to give thanks to the people and companies that without their product and services, I could not have presented such a package as you now have before you.

I want to thank Microsoft Office for the tools they included in their software packages that allowed me to document and manipulate all of my Microsoft **Word** writings, my Microsoft **Excel** spreadsheets, my Microsoft **Access** databases and my Microsoft **Outlook** correspondences to put things together. Also, all my finished album cover artwork was done with the sub-programs included in Microsoft **Word,** like **WordArt** and the, **Pictures manipulation** program.

I want to thank the free, open-source, GNU Image Manipulation Program, (**GIMP 2.10.8**) of which I have come to love, although, I have barely scratched the surface of what this free, Adobe Photoshop - Photo & Design like software can do, but it has saved me at least, $599.88 or the guilt I might have felt had I tried to pirate the Adobe software. Well done folks, well done indeed.

I want to thank Florian Heidenreich, an Indie Software Developer living in Dresden with a background in professional software development for over twenty years, for his "**MP3TAG**" free software, of which I am so humbly grateful to for the digital tagging of all my Wav and MP3 files, (songs). Over the years I have come to think of Florian as a good friend who has been with me on my journey, helping me to accomplish great things through his simple but magnificent program. Again, well done indeed.

Big thanks to my son Brian's best friend, (and my friend) Jamie who volunteered to work on my web page and is in the process of getting my web page, **(www.LordBaldwin.com)** up to date, in spite of the fact that he has a new job, a fairly new marriage to Jenna, and a little two-year-old boy to balance. This web page is very important to me as the possible face and liaisons to the Lord Baldwin Happenings. Jamie and Jenna continue to be inspirational and positive, with upbeat ideas and encouraging suggestions to make the Lord Baldwin web pages better.

Thanks to the people at "**https://combinepdf.com/**" who's free online software helped me to manipulate and combine my varied PDF files. They also saved me from the guilt I would have felt, had I pirated that Adobe software, also because of their free online service, I didn't have to pay $449.00 to the Adobe people for their Acrobat Pro software. Thank you, "CombinePDF.com."

I want to thank VoidTools.com for their Everything software which is the best file manager ever. No matter how the files in my Windows 10 computer are indexed, Microsoft file manager takes forever and many times it comes up blank; it's a joke. But when I really need to find something or a directory something is in, the Everything software is the best, and can scan all the files in my computer hard drives, in two or three seconds.

I now wish to thank the very excellent people at DistroKid who helped me to get my music and song distributed and out throughout the world. I can't begin to express how grateful I am to finally have a chair to the world stage, and in spite of the number's rollercoaster of listeners, to have the ability to have people in Korea and Germany and India and Brazil and Norway and Japan and Australia and the United Kingdom be able to stream my material at any time and any place through Spotify and other streaming facilities is just so awesome.

Thank you again folks so much for everything you've done for me. You guys rock!

As you can imagine, there are many other unsung heroes out there that I want to thank them for their help in making this new endeavor possible right now. And here is the shout out to my lovely best friend, Diane who unconditionally loves me and continues to believe in me, and inspires me to write the many love songs for her that she so richly and honorably deserves.

And here is my call out to all my children and their children. Please know that I dedicate all of this thing I do to all of you and again, to Diane, with my most sincere love and devotion.

I hope whomever you are, that you can find enjoyment in these pages of this documentation of these next nine albums along with their corresponding songs.

Yours Indubitably,

LORD BALDWIN

3

SPECIAL NOTE TO MY
FAMILY

I decided that I'd like to say something special, just to you; my children and to my children's children, (my grandchildren), so here goes,... You all know me and know that I love music,... It fills me up with happiness and can help me get out of bad places like when I'm feeling annoyed or angry about something,... Music has healing powers that can mend your soul and repair your broken heart. I want you to know that music can have the same medicinal powers on you too, if you wish.

You may or may not have pondered about this thought, but I want to address this here and now,... There are things in our being that were passed on from generation to generation through our DNA,... things passed on from our mothers and from our fathers that help define the attributes that comprise our physical and chemical makeup,...

New scientific studies now suggest that some of our memories, fears, and behaviors are passed down genetically through generations from our ancestors,... Recent studies done by epigenetic scientists and researchers even suggest that we receive loads of genetic memories from our parents, grandparents, and further ancestors, in an instinctive effort by their DNA to better prepare ours for difficult experiences that they have faced, such as fear, disease, or trauma,... These epigenetic scientists also study how genes are inherited and the changes to those genetics that we exhibit, even when those changes are not essential to our DNA,... These changes can be affected or recalled by our experiences, age, environment, and health.

It came to me one night a couple of months ago that within this receiving of coded genetic DNA that we were all given, through the transferal of genes from our fathers, mothers, grandmothers, grandfathers, etc., we also received special gifts and talents that we, if we so discover, could use and magnify,... Let me be even more plain on this; our Heavenly Father has instilled within us, many gifts and talents, expecting us to discover them and to magnify those talents to accomplish great things while here on this earth.

I believe that examining our heritage can help us to identify some of those gifts and talents,... I don't have too much documentation to extrapolate data from the past because I only vaguely knew my great grandmother Viola Snook, on my mother's side, who, played harmonica in her teens in a band in 1885 and continued playing her whole life till her passing in 1970, but I can say with a certainty that both my grandparents on my mother's side, my mother, who played piano and early on transposed musical documents for my father, father, who played accordion, organ and piano professionally in the early 50s,... and they all inherited and used their special gift of music that were passed down to them,...

Some of **our** ancestors, like my mother and father, knew that they had this gift of music and they shared it with the world as they went about their lives doing what they did,... some of our other ancestors got busy with life and maybe magnified other talents that they recognized early on,... It doesn't mean they didn't have the gift of music, it just meant that that particular gift might not have been discovered or might not have been as important to them as other pursuits,...

Okay, so where am I going with this,... I came to the realization that not long after discovering that I had these special talents and the gift of music, I began to move quickly forward in my understanding of how chord progressions worked, and it all seemed to happen logically in my head,... There is no substitute for **practice**,... but I found that as I was practicing, the tediousness and redundancies did not bother me at all and I found a kind of joy in my eventual progress,...

I had wanted to be a singer/songwriter for a long time, but there was something in my DNA that told me, 'of course you can do that — you and your ancestorial line were instilled with musical talents from our Heavenly Father *many* generations ago with the gift of music' and therefore, you were born with the gift of music,... and how cool is that?

Long story short, you, my children and grandchildren also inherited my DNA which means that you too have these special talents and the gift of music,...

IF YOU WISH, you only need to search for and discover them within, to magnify your powers,... I say, *if you wish*, because not every-one, even those blessed with these talents will feel the need or want to amplify the music powers within,... There is a price to pay for becoming a musician,... beyond your special gifts, as with everything in life, and for even the most gifted of artists and writers, as mentioned before, there is a basic prerequisite and necessity for you to **practice**, and prac-tice and practice even more to get to a higher level of proficiency,...

Still, it is your choice to go in that direction or not, but please know this; not everyone has the special talents and the gift of music like you do,... and unless you hate music and everything about it, which I'm pretty sure is not happening in your DNA, it costs you nothing but your time and effort to explore this fascinating world of music.

One more thing; your talent, that music gift we're talking about is powerful and very much like magic. It should not be used inappropri-ately. You should not use your powers to hurt others or to puff yourself up and be full of yourself, or to gain advantage at someone else's ex-pense, or to hurt someone that is less talented than you. It doesn't mean you can't be competitive at times or that after you've reached a level of proficiency that you can't go out and make money with your talents. There are many good people in this world that use their musical powers to pay their rent and to buy food. That is okay. You need to value your musical powers and know that if you want the powers to stay, if you want your musical talents to grow, you will need to do it in the spirit of kindness and love and you need to be good.

Now, look inside your being and find your powers and magnify your talents, whether they be music or writing or art or something else,... Those talents are all there, you just have to find them and use them wisely. Please know that I love you, and wish you happy hunting.

4

10 - HEAVEN - 1992

5

NOTES ABOUT THE COVERS

The original album cover was very colorfully done and was from one of Maxfield Parrish's prints called "***Daybreak***," (seen below).

I chose this for multiple reasons; the settings and angelic-like scenery looked so stoically and heavenly, also, the two people, from their comfortably contented appearance, their unwistful disposition and demeanor, looking like they were in heaven, and lastly, it was one of the pictures on the wall in my Grandma Snook's apartment when Richie and I stayed with her in 1963. Obviously, there was no doubt that this cover had to go.

Afterwards I was not so enamored with my choices especially because I have a condition called, pareidolia which is a psychological phenomenon that causes people to see patterns in a random stimulus, and in my case, I assign human characteristics and mostly faces to objects,...

And looking at the lettering above the clouds the "H" and the "V" or maybe the "E" and the "A" seem to form eyes above a not-so-welcoming mouth; like maybe an angry being looking back at you,...

Crazy, right? But the album was already published and a done deal before I caught this,...

and sorry now for you if I've ended up putting those ideas in your head,...

you probably won't be able to see it any other way, anymore.

6

HEAVEN

Heaven
Living The Streets
Make Your Move
Back In The Arms Of The Lord, Again
The Barriers We've Made
Tomorrow Never Comes
Back In The Navy
Drifting Apart
Gunning For The Kid

"Heaven," Copyright © - July of 1992, All Rights Reserved

7

Heaven

Heaven, seems like heaven,
all these days we've spent together.
All the years you've given to me,
with devotion, almost heaven.
Heaven, seems like heaven,
with our children growing with us.
And the love you're giving to them,
makes our family bright like heaven.
Heaven, seems like heaven,
with us all sealed to each other.
As we learn about forever,
to be together like in heaven.
Heaven, seems like heaven,
as we work towards exaltation.
Fills my heart with such a soft peace,
Happiness shines bright like heaven.
Heaven, seems like heaven,
with our purpose just before us.
All this love and understanding,
brings our family close to heaven.

8

Living The Streets

Tear down the buildings on First and Main,
only going to put good people out of a place to stay.
Town rising up with offices clean and warm,
taking out doorways needed to shelter the storm.

Gleaning the alleyway with I don't know who.
Out of luck, out of money, with nothing else to do.
Bottle of wine crashing through my head,
looks like this park bench here is going to be my bed.

I just want some sleep, well, I just want some sleep,
I just want some peace, but I'm living the streets.

Ten years ago, I fell down in this hell.
Hardly remember now why it was I fell.
People looking down like I'm some kind of freak,
especially when I'm asking for money or something to eat.

Had my rise and fall years ago in the rat race war.
I got no plans to go back there anymore.

I don't need no preaching or judging what's wrong or right,
I just want a warm, dry place to stay the night.

I just want some sleep, well, I just want some sleep,
I could use some peace, but I'm living the streets.

I never saw the signs or the walls of the lines I crossed,
only know I'm stranded here in the land of the lost.
You can ignore me hoping I might go away,
and you tear down our building on First and Main.

I just want some sleep, but I can't get no sleep,
I just want some peace, but I'm living the streets.

9

Make Your Move

Too many days have passed without us resolving,
the problems still in doubt.
We've talked and worked things out before,
but this time I'm locked out.
I'm waiting, ready to take your hand
should a change come over you.
There's not much left that I can do until you make your move.
I got involved, to bring you back, to where we were at first.
I gave you space to work it out but it seems that things got worse.
We can't communicate or touch
when there's something left to prove.
Looking away and hoping soon You will make your move.
The loving smile, the passion glance, the gentle knowing touch,
are all a part of relationships that say and mean so much.
Little things don't mean the same, when all the magic's lost.
All the hopes and dreams are dashed
When the lines can not be crossed.
To wonder what it all was for is to lose the cause we knew.
but I'll be here when you come back to me
and make your move.

10

Back In The Arms Of The Lord, Again

I remember the morning, just like it was today.
Everything reminds me how much I'd want to stay.
And I looked out the window, the sun was shinning down,
and I thought, "What a day for my family to be around."

Everything falls to what could or should have been,
but I'm back here now in the arms of the Lord, again.

It's taken too much time, to understand why.
Just a young child waiting here in this line.
All my brothers and my sisters, looking to me,
how could they ever know what was soon to be?

My Father and my Mother's heart were broken to then,
but I'm back here in the arms of the Lord, once again.

So much I wanted to say, so much I needed to do,
and yet, it all comes down to what we already knew.

There's a time to be here, a time we'll have to leave,
and a time to know, a time to believe.

Your heart-felt feelings will all soon mend,
and I'm here back now in the arms of the Lord, again.

It'll never be easy, it's hard to understand,
even when you believe in the Lord and his hand.
But families are forever, I'm prepared to wait,
and I can not cry for the joy's too much to save.

I can only think of all of those friends
and now I'm here back in the arms of the Lord, again.
Back in the Lord's arms again.

The Barriers We've Made

I'm running out of time; there's so much I need to say.
You're going through the motions that you'll soon be gone away.
I need to let you know you're fun to be around,
and that I'm hoping we might share some common ground.
But we don't know each other beyond all the games we played,
so how can we get through all the barriers we've made.
Beyond the games and the lies beyond the lost, trusting eyes,
there is a common ground where we can make a trade.
Within the ever-growing trust as we explore below the crust
and break down all of the barriers we've made.
We're running out of time to put together something real.
I sense beyond the motions that there's something that you feel.
I want that you should know how and why I feel this way,
but the words are all beyond me and the actions out of place.
Though we don't know each other, decisions must be weighed,
and we must try to get through all the barriers we've made.
Beyond words and ideals, all the unheard heart appeals,
there is a growing hope and foundations being laid.
Beyond the superficial plane, there is a chance to try again
and break down all of the barriers we've made.

12

Tomorrow Never Comes

Chase those dreams for an eternity,
convince yourself of their validity,
but don't be surprised if they die out in the sun.
If you wait for someday or somehow,
and don't get involved right here and now
you may have today, but tomorrow never comes.
Too much hope and I was the slave
to wait for miracles to save
me and my own from rotting in the slums.
I've learned the bitter and the sweet
and I believe in now and me,
I love my dreams, but tomorrow never comes.

Tomorrow never comes, tomorrow only runs away.
Lost dreams of why and how,
hey, we've only got here and now, today.

Look closely there between the lines,
see the truth from all the signs
no need to grovel there for all the crumbs.

Take inventory what you need,
and fight for all that you believe
today is here, but tomorrow never comes.

I used to march the grand parade
and gambled all my time away
till I was left there hanging by my thumbs.
As time dragged on and began to wear,
I saw the real world waiting there
like a future, but tomorrow never comes.

Tomorrow never comes, tomorrow only runs away.
Lost dreams of why and how,
hey, we've only got here and now, today.

Chase those dreams and shoot the moon,
sing yourself a trusting tune
but kiss that dream goodbye before you're done.
I've learned the bitter and the sweet
but I believe something in me
knows of today, but tomorrow never comes.

Tomorrow never comes, tomorrow only runs away.
Lost dreams of why and how, hey,
we've only got here and now, today.
Tomorrow never comes.

13

Back In The Navy

Joined the navy in nineteen thirty seven,
things were kind of shaky but the traveling was heaven.
Stood in the rain, waiting for the truck,
my duty almost over and all that time to shuck.
I remember when I left, the trees were swaying.
I can still hear her voice as she was saying,

"Oh, while you're away, don't you hesitate
to write to me and to communicate.
Oh, but please keep in touch, because I love you so much,
you know you're my crutch and I can hardly wait
for you to get back home, so get back home,
home so get back home, home to me."

Spent four years and now it's time to return.
Almost Christmas time back home in Auburn.
Sitting in the station, staring at the clock.
Suddenly the place went wild with everyone in shock.
Then they called all the available men,
and I was back in the navy again.

I remember when I left the band was playing
and the tears within her eyes as she was saying,

"Oh, and while you're away, don't you hesitate
to write to me and to communicate.
Oh, but please keep in touch, because I love you so much,
you know you're my crutch and I can hardly wait
for you to get back home, so get back home,
home so get back home, home to me."

14

Drifting Apart

We made our choices, within our life,
put things off for some other time.
Compromise for all we want,
and put the priorities out front.
Promises from words that run,
I wait for you, but you never come.

And we've drifted apart from too many times
of letting things go and not speaking our minds.
Just letting the small things tear into the heart,
till we're miles away and drifting apart.

I see the smile, from her warm face,
in a different time and a different place.
I remember the fun, the talks at night,
the passion, the purpose that must have been right.
Actions speak louder than words passed round,
you lead me on, then you let me down.

And we've drifted apart from too many times

of letting things go and not speaking our minds.
Just letting the small things tear into the heart,
till we're miles away and drifting apart.

We haven't gone so far that I can't still see your light,
but if we wait much longer,
we'll sail out of each other's sight.

We've drifted apart but you're still in view,
reach out as I throw this lifeline to you.
If we could just think and act as one heart,
we wouldn't be miles away and drifting apart.

15

Gunning For The Kid

In my younger years I ran the jagged course.
Always in some kind of trouble with authority or force.
Fighting off oppression of the mighty and the strong,
standing up against
what I perceived was wrong.

I made a lot of enemies pushing back all of the jerks,
my fists would speak at times when reason didn't work.
Seems they were always after me even for things I never did,
lurking in the shadows
and gunning for the kid.

Oppression has a way of never leaving me alone,
my need for social justice seems to always set the tone.
Always bucking a system that's trying to take me out
and them a bit upset,
their authority in doubt.

No diplomacy or tact, against overwhelming odds,
doing it the hard way and being the under-dog.

Rattlesnakes are coiled to strike me from the grid,
but I'm loaded and ready
when they come gunning for the kid.

I keep a watchful eye for those who lay in wait.
I know they're out there after me harboring some hate.
From the officer in hiding beyond the next bend
to the bureaucrat who'd trip me up
while posing as a friend.

Not to mention in the shadows of my mistakes and doubt
is Lucifer and his legions hoping to take me out.
I remain a moving target with my home ground safely hid.
Both guns drawn and ready
for those gunning for the kid.

16

MEMOIRS & NOTES - 10 - 'HEAVEN'

Heaven

1991) – Family has always been important to me, even before I was still in the process of creating one. It was so wonderful having our first child, Loren, who filled in a missing part of the puzzle that helped make our lives so wonderful. Lori, with her distinctive perceptiveness and ability for drawing and later, painting, and later, her eye for using a camera was the perfect beginning and model of our children to follow and learn from. Then came Chet III or, Chet boy, and when he arrived, never did you see a kid seem to get it so quickly, and I mean he could figure things out without being shown how, probably why he was so good at everything he tried; baseball, basketball, Boy Scouts, and with the advent of both genders interacting, things changed all over again in our family. And next there was Liz, an artist from the beginning and an altogether different personality from Lori and Chet. Liz was my little thinker too; but in a different way than Chet, Liz had the ability to make herself a part of whatever was going on with anybody and every-body loved her and got along with her, especially, the next baldwin, Meridith; my little entertainer with an instinctive sense of comedic timing, and any raised surface was a stage for her to get up on to dance, and throw in her genuine but unpretentious sense of humor, she was our entertainer and her overwhelming need for fairness in everything and all family matters, she was a force to recon with. She was followed by Benjamin, captivated by toy cars and trucks like hot wheels, and even at two years old, like his sisters Lori and Liz, had a distinctive eye for creating art, and later a musician, (Trumpet and Baritone and even Tuba) and later, a computer enthusiast with strong math skills, then Stephen, good with all games including Chess, multiple board and card games and later a musician, (Trumpet and guitar), and also a song-writer. Spencer comes next, and he is just a ball of concentrated fire and energy trapped in his temporal body, then comes Christopher, the thinker and ever a self-proclaimed, I'm a one-of-the-in-crowd, socialite, ever being involved in his older brother's businesses.

And then comes our 1990 surprise, Allison, coming around the time I had lost my Job at JW and gone back to school, Allison had an ability to feel someone's inter-turmoil, she sense they were having problems or issues and she could interact with them and help them to feel good again, (a good talent), and Alli was followed four years later by Brian, who has the innate ability to accomplish anything he sets his mind to, and also another musician, (Trumpet and guitar and keyboards) and also a songwriter. Being close to each other over the years has helped make our group a discerning and caring family.

Side Note:

I loved the idea of being a father and took the responsibilities seriously. I also reaped the rewards of the joy and happiness of being married to this wonderful woman that was not only the best mom but a great companion that shared my joy in children and accepted my career and financial shortcomings, and stood by me in my low times of inadequacies and failures and reveled with me and my successes in music and verse.

To me, this was like heaven. I had lofty plans for the future that never materialized, but the children all turned out magnificently. They all love and take care of each other. And I believe it was because of our commitment to this stewardship of parenthood and because of our joy in being in our home, working at the endearing job of being a mother, a father, a brother, a sister; a family member all loving and helping each other.

Another Side Note:

We in this life existence, no matter what our beliefs, have our preconceived notions and ideas of what heaven is to us, and I would guess that even most people in whatever walk of life with or without religious persuasions might still have different concepts or perceptions of what that is all about amongst themselves. As many people that interact with the Baldwins and as many of you may have gathered or surmised from some of my previous writings, we are members of the Church of Jesus Christ of Latter-Day Saints, or LDS abbreviated and or "Mormon," of which has, in these subsequent days, taken on by some in the church members to be stigmatized in a negative sort of demeanor. This association for me in particular has had its positive as well as negative effects and ultimate outcomes.

Yet Another Side Note:

The best thing about raising kids under the overall umbrella of the

LDS church was and is that the church is very family centered and an excellent resource with tools and helps for the raising of my children, and that good, positive influence was truly a blessing. I saw my children's interactions, at least up to high school, to be a most positive influence on their developing character and I have watched them ALL grow up to be wonderful, outstanding people, good citizens of and for the communities, states, country and world that they live in while contributing to the wellbeing of their sociological, economical, spiritual, ecological and environmental issues and challenges encompassing and affecting their lives. The fact that most of my kids have chosen not to continue being active in the church at this time is a deep-seated but ongoing hardship, more so to Diane than me. It seemed that every time we heard of one of our kid's friends going off to a mission it would sadden Diane and it would be days before that cloud would lift from her outward manner. And I have felt the anguish of her inner sadness when yet another child stopped going to church. Still, they're all good people with the ability to be free thinkers using their free agency for good. We only hope that we have taught them correct principals so that they might govern themselves and their families in a loving and righteous way.

Living The Streets

(1990) – During one of my visits to Portland in the late 80s I was going up Burnside Street in downtown Portland to visit our old apartment (the Estell Apartments), and check out how the neighborhood had changed, and I noticed a lot of construction going on in the area. In the past for as long as I could remember, there was a lot of transient population living in that area, especially Third & Burnside; where the city fathers, wanting to get rid of the homeless, transient population that congregated around there, decided to tear down all the old buildings and rebuild the wharf area to something more modern. Unfortunately, there was nowhere left for the down and out to go and be. And I was lamenting the choices of those in charge that take little regard for the people they relocate or put out of residence.

Allison who was a newborn at the time, was asleep in my bed, so after I woke up, two in the morning, I went into Elizabeth and Meridith's bedroom to write the poem for this song and after reconstructed the words, the tune and ultimately the whole song fell intoo place in about an hour. Liz woke up and asked me what I was doing and I just said "I'm writing a song." This wasn't the first time and would not be the last, and she quickly got disinterested and went back to sleep.

Make Your Move

(1991) – It can be implied that when there is a problem and there is a desire to fix that problem, someone needs to make the first move. I am not good with names over a long time passed, but there was this tall woman that I knew while working at the Parks department that I bump into periodically and she would always say hi to me, by name and I had a hard time remembering her name but as she's walking away, she again reveals that her name is Nancy. Anyway, Nancy, who was single, was going through her midlife crisis along with the problematic circumstances that her boyfriend was vacillating over commitment. She was ready to jump in and he, after being married and divorced twice, was less than receptive to this type of obligation. She of course was frustrated and their relationship went downhill from there. For a few months, silly things from both camps would cause arguments and sometime later, she was out on one of our 15-minute walks where she said that her relationship was on hold and she was just waiting for him to make the move, hence these lyrics or this poem.

Back In The Arms Of The Lord, Again

(1992) – Perhaps more than any other song, this is the one I play the least. Not like my third and fourth albums that I have a hard time with, because they didn't meet up to my expectations, no, this one is special, this one comes way too close to home and heart. I Still can not listen to this without breaking down and crying.

The lyrics are written from my son Christopher's perspective and point of view and is about the day he left us. It talks about his day and time, his looking at us after his death and his acceptance and peace found in the hereafter. Not too many weeks before his passing on May 15, 1992,

Chris-Boy & His Posse

Elizabeth was playing around with a tape recorder and recorded a small conversation with him. I included this tape entry as well as overlaying the music theme at the end with, at least to me, stunning, heartbreaking results. Right after I wrote the words to this poem, Diane asked me if I had been inspired, perhaps by his spirit, to write the words and compose this poem with the way the words came out. I told her then that I wasn't sure. I didn't feel any great movement swell to be overcome by the spirit, so I didn't know, but after a few years passed, I guess I'm no longer sure that I wasn't inspired. I'd like to think that perhaps, at the time, I was looking for some earth-shaking, awesome, experience, and perhaps in my grieving state it softly came, but maybe my heart was just too broken at the time but I just didn't recognize it to feel the gentle promptings of the spirit.

Side Note:

After Chris's passing, there was no escape for me and my family from the fallout of my *third* **BIG HURT**. I was broke, unemployed, empty and lost when this happened. Diane was holding it together better than me, good that she was, keeping up with the rollercoaster of emotions all of the kids were going through while I locked myself away in my bedroom trying to make sense of what to do now. People would say, "Well at least you still have eight other kids to fall back on," like Chris was just another carbon copy of one of the others. The thing that knocked me out of my unhappiness state was when I got called into the Black Lake Elementary principal's office about an incident that happened. Apparently, on the way to or back from school on the school bus there was an unsensitive (or belligerently nasty) older sixth-grade boy, characteristically a bully and frequent tormenter, that thought with his apparent larger size, older age and warped social status, (a feared bully), that he would be safe and that it would be fun to taunt and tease Ben and Stephen about losing their little brother, Christopher. Ben, who was ten at the time, wasted no time scrambling over two or three sets of bus seats full of other kids and immediately started clobbering the boy who was surprised that Ben was not intimated by the size and stature differences, and maybe surprised that his wickedness would foster such a reaction, but the driver of the bus had to stop and pull Ben off of the bully, who tried but failed to fight back, was now sporting a bloody nose and was fearfully struggling just to keep Ben from pummeling him. Ben was asked to stay home the next day, (the bully was suspended from school for a longer period), but said that he needed to go to school to protect Stephen in case something like this happened again. I told Stephen he could take the day off with Ben and they were both happy. On a different note, I think Ben told me that, although the bully steered clear of the Baldwins all together, the bully must have had other issues at home, because he did not seem to learn from his episode but went back to intimidating the weaker younger kids and harassing and terrorizing kids in the shadows at the school.

Another Side Note:

If the memories and the feelings of the big loss aren't enough hearing

Christopher's voice interacting with Liz's followed by the lonesome harmonica and the slow guitar strums at the end of this song along with with the whisperings, "Mom, Dad,... I'm home again" always gets to me,... makes me cry,..,

Barriers We've Made

(1992) – In my childhood I watched the animosity and enmity of my Scarbrough grandparents as it grew more distant, as I grew older. In my innocent, secret wishes, I had hoped that they could reconcile their differences and get back together again. Neither one remarried, and, although grandma did kind of have a boyfriend, it was superficial and platonic at most. The thing was,

L to R: Grandpa Scarbrough, Era & Harold Snook, Grandma
Scarbrough, Aunt Ruby & Great Grandma Snook

I knew grandpa for his shortcomings like drinking and smoking and gambling, but that perspective of mine was from grandma's perspective, not his. And I knew grandma from her need to be a good Seventh Day Adventist, (SDA), her ongoing kindnesses and support to my mother and to her grandkids, but she was also a hypochondriac that begged for your attention and to have you feel sorry for her and she complained more than she should have. Grandma wanted a more stable family life, and a Christian-like relationship, like she saw in her other SDA members. Grandpa wanted the fun-loving girl he married to return and accept him for what he was, not what she thought he should be. Arguably, grandpa and grandma broke up because each wanted the other to be do or be something they could not. Now, I'm not sure how she otherwise felt about him, but I know I never heard him say a single bad word about her and I'm sure he died still loving her. Two people can change their world if they want to.

Anyway, as time passed it seemed easier to accept things the way they were and not only let the barriers continue to exist, but to fortify them and justify their existence. Still, I always wished that they could have resolved their differences, fallen back in love, and be together again.

Tomorrow Never Comes

(1991) – Sometimes pursuing today and dealing with today is better than hoping for tomorrow. I have eaten the elephant many times for many different occasions. I have learned to bide my time and work for the reward that comes bye and bye, but sometimes I think it would be better to jump ahead and go for broke. I'm not saying to eat, drink and be merry for tomorrow we die, but I am saying that sometimes we spend all of our energy and dreams working on some future that is happening right now and we let it pass, waiting for it to come around again, but the reality to the whole farce is that it never will.

Side Note:

My mindset for writing this was that for years, I would look in the mirror to see the real me, but instead I would see the guy with the facial blemishes, or the man getting fatter all the time, or the guy with his receding hairline, or the image of the guy that made me feel inadequate for his failed efforts to provide for his family. In contrast I was always shooting for that guy, the other guy that would be clear skinned, that would be thinner, that had good teeth and good hair, the guy that was making it—the good provider for his family; always looking for the tomorrow that never comes instead of loving that reflection of the guy that did all he could to keep his family going, nurtured with love.

Another Side Note:

This song marked a milestone in my approach to a new song with the use of the new Yamaha keyboard which opened up new possibilities for me to branch out beyond the standard necessary percussion to experiment with some of my new voices available there. And this song, "Tomorrow Never Comes" also steered me into a few other directions to escape the limited folk-rock sound and start expressing myself in and with the In-House or In-Home Jazz that, over the years, has only increased and magnified.

Back In The Navy

(1976) – This concept stemmed from someone John talked about years ago when he returned from Naples. Seems there was this sailor that had just gotten out of the navy getting back in the states and was in some railway station getting ready to be transported to his home when the news of Pearl Harbor came over the loud speakers at the station. He turned back around, reenlisted and served honorably during World War II, and then became a career naval officer. The story, which I had heard in 1962, stayed with me all those years and eventually became a song.

Drifting Apart

(1991) – This was written right about the time I lost my job with the Washington State Parks Department and I was not communicating well with anyone. Diane and I got into some argument about something that seemed important at the time, but anyway, I took it personally and we stopped talking to each other for a while, and this poem materialized. It just takes a small disparity to make a big difference. And like someone that misses church one week for a good reason, and then misses church the next week, and then the third week comes around and you may not feel exceptionally motivated to go, because you've altered your customs, traditions, conventions of behavior; you feel justified. So it is with communicating to your loved one. It starts with someone getting annoyed with the other, then the silent treatment, then the thought process kicks in where there is a need for justice and the silence is substituted for forgiveness instead of the other way around, and after a while, because you've altered your customs traditions conventions of love, you may not feel exceptionally motivated to get back together, you may feel justified in continuing down this darker road of uncertainty and hurt.

Gunning For The Kid

(1991) –This is about the life and times of me perhaps, but it has been suggested, and I cannot argue, that my brother Ray is in here too. Questioning authority has always been my mode of operation but Ray seems to have taken it up a few notches and lives by the rule of "fight the power" emphatically. More than me, (because of the lifestyle he has chosen to live), he has the world coming at him from all sides and he has learned to take on all newcomers and old foes, and he usually wins. How does he do it? He does his homework and he knows what he's talking about, sometimes more than the authorities he's taking on. He is aggressive and takes a strong defensive stand, especially because he is usually right and he knows it, he also has a very strong motivation for self-preservation, and if they come after him, they will usually fall because he knows he is right and that he has the laws on his side. But this is not always true. Sometimes he is right but the system can be corrupt and cruel, exercising unrighteousness, which he has to fight even more so now, and sometimes he takes on the mantle of the renegade, running from whatever, sometimes even the law.

Side Note:
There was this story that was related to me that happened one Friday afternoon while Ray was in Portland, at the courthouse, hassling the

state insurance companies over his back injuries that he had incurred at a construction site where they were building apartments and a large twenty-foot-long by nine-feet high, skeletal 2x4 structured wall fell on him. In spite of good documentation, Ray had a lot of problems with the insurance companies paying up and more problems with their inadequate coverage; all of which was putting him and his family in a bind. He came into the courtroom with a briefcase full of documentation that even the insurance company's lawyers didn't have. Essentially, he proved to them that they were indeed negligent and the courts ruled in his favor.

Ray was parked outside the courthouse in a parking meter spot, and his time had expired on the meter. Because he was already in the rears with other parking tickets, when the meter maid ticketed him, she had the vehicle flagged and it was towed away. He came out or the courtroom happy, only to see his vehicle gone and he became livid over the whole circumstance. He found out where the vehicle, a beat-up gray Chevy Love pickup, had been towed to and then he went to the tow yard. When he got there, he argued with these two huge goons; (the towing people), who announced that the tow service would cost Ray two hundred and fifty dollars, and they told him authoritatively that they were closing up the wrecking yard for the weekend and he wouldn't be able to get his vehicle until Monday adding another fifty dollars a day, making his total four hundred dollars. When Ray calmly told them that he would write them a check right there on the spot, they agreed to let him go to his truck to get out his checkbook. Somewhere on his walk into their yard and getting to his vehicle,

Ray decides he has had enough and gets into his vehicle and starts it up and quickly starts to drive off and out of their lot. The two goons start to pull the big gates shut but it is too late as Ray maneuvers around one side of the left gate opening and through the right-side opening.

Ray has escaped, but the two-tow people, now livid, jump into their five-ton towing truck and begin to pursue the escaped vehicle and its owner. All through downtown Portland, on a Friday night with all the heavy traffic congestion, Ray is driving his Chevy Love pickup like he's in a race, and he's being closely followed by the angry tow-truck people. After about a half an hour of ducking down alleys and going through red lights,

Ray looks behind him and realizes he has lost them. He did have to go and pay the parking fines sometime later, but he never heard from that towing company again. Oh, those were good times,... and did I mention that he paid the parking tickets with part of the money he got from the insurance settlement?

17

11 - A LONG WAY FROM MY HOME - 1992

18

NOTES ABOUT THE
COVERS

Except for the lettering which was lost in the document conversions, here we have the original album cover. I did spent hours, (believe it or not), getting the fonts to look just right. The picture you see here is my Grandpa Scarbrough, in his later years, picture taken maybe mid-60s, leaning on the back-quarter panel of what I believe to be, his 2 door, 1953-55, super 88 Oldsmobile. I loved that car from the first time I watched him turn on the radio and the antenna automatically lifted out of the chassis. As you know (or will know), I took care of him in some of his last years, and the story goes, I was going to get his car when he passed away. Kind of a big deal to me. But when he did pass away in Redmond Oregon, at the end of 1968, he had incurred a lot of doctor's bills and he owed the place he was living at the time, the Redmond Hotel, rent and back rent money. So, away the car (and my dreams) went.

Side Note:

After my mother divorced my dad when I was five, the new person she married was a guy we're gonna call, Senior. Senior married my mother with the expectations that a fully-paid-for house came with her; a house

61

that Grandpa Scarbrough bought for my mother and father, and much to Senior's unhappiness, Grandma Scarbrough who was living in the house and had squatters' rights, not only let Senior know that he would not be getting the house after all but refused to even let him into the house. Things for us stepchildren went downhill from there and never got better. Grandpa Scarbrough was my only true father figure when I was growing up. I loved the way he treated his daughter; so much love and respect, and when I was a kid, he was perhaps the only man that ever treated me with love and took the time to listen to me and seemed interested in what my boy's life was all about.

But Grandpa Scarbrough, he was just the best.

19

A LONG WAY FROM MY HOME

A Long Way From My Home
A Shadow Of A Doubt
It Ain't Gonna Happen Tonight
I Am The Fool
Who's In Charge Of It All
Somewhere In Between
The Yodeler
Tumbleweed

20

A Long Way From My Home

I was a cowboy and I roamed the open range,
but I stayed too long and I got caught up in the change.
My friends all caught the vision and the first horse out of town,
me, I was the fool not to see and stayed around.
I lost my job when the railroad came down from the north.
There wasn't any need for driving cattle anymore.
I remember standing out there, looking up and down the road,
wondering as the winter fell, which way I was going to go.

I was a long way from my home, and I'd never been this alone.
I got nowhere left that I can go anymore;
I'm just a long way from my home.

Moved to the mountains about the spring of 23,
heard a man could make his fortune cutting down them trees.
So, from sun up to sun down we worked,
bucking trees fifteen feet across.
The way things figured way back then, nobody'd ever feel the loss.
Soon we stripped the land and moved up on the bluff.
A wild and cold winter set in and made things for us real tough.

So, I traded in my mountain boots and laid my buck saw down,
looking for my life and times drifting from town to town.

Just a long way from my home, and I'd never been this alone.
I got nowhere left that I can go anymore;
I'm just a long way from my home.

I moved to the city but I didn't stay very long.
Got a job pushing a cat on the coast of Oregon.
Work was sure and steady and the pay was mighty fine,
but everything just fell apart with the crash of twenty-nine.
I lost job, my savings, even lost my home.
We were thrown out in the streets with no prospects and no hope.
Friends and neighbors broken, were too poor to up and give.
Family looking in me, wondering how we're going to live.

I was a long way from my home, and I'd never been this alone.
I got nowhere left that I can go anymore,
I'm just a long way from my home.

Ain't no telling what a desperate man might do
when he gets caught up in a fire and wants to climb out of the stew.
I fell in with the wrong people that started dragging me down,
before I know'd it, there I was in jail outside of town.
Spent near eighteen months before they let me out.
I was broke and destitute, and plagued with constant doubt.
Folks all over the county saying, "Hey, we ain't got no jobs,
but anyway, we ain't in no habit of hiring ex-cons."

I was a long way from my home, and I'd never been this alone.
Got nowhere left that I can go anymore;
I'm just a long way from my home.

Been many years since I been back around Cheyenne,

always want to go back but something always falls into my plans.
I heard from passing people that the town has up and changed,
reckon kind of like my life, nothing ever stays the same.
Old cowboys on wooden sidewalks talking about old times,
been replaced by department stores and advertising signs.
All the people I remember have all died or moved away,
don't imagine anyone there would remember me anyway.

Just a long way from my home, and I'd never been this alone.
I got nowhere left that I can go anymore,
I'm just a long way from my home.

Now as my days wind down I'm stuck in this hotel room.
Most the time too sick to leave, even just to get some food.
This emphysema is closing in from too many dusty roads,
but my Seagram Seven and Chesterfields
are holding me for the load.
As all my life and times roll by me like an arcade,
regrets and afterthoughts like hindsight start to fade.
Thoughts of the hereafter, God and heaven I hardly had,
I can only hope now that my good out weighs my bad.

I'm just a long way from my home, and I never,
I ain't never been this alone.
I got nowhere left that I can go anymore; I'm just a long way,
I'm just a long way—just a long way from my home.

21

A Shadow Of A Doubt

I know, we've been so long together, me and you.
I know, there's so much that we've gone through.
Time passes, we go on as problems
are swept out of sight,
The questions, unanswered
are never brought in the light.
I know that lately, at times I been feeling shut out.
I see behind your eyes; a shadow of a doubt.

I know, people change, fall in and out of love.
I know, we've had our share
of problems to think of.
Time passes, we get on with the playing of the game.
although it's like nothing's changed,
nothing is the same.
I know we want to believe the best of what it's about,
it's hard to just continue with a shadow of a doubt.

You think I'm sulking around, keeping something hid.
I think you don't love me for something I once did.

We need to communicate,
to bring back the close that's gone.
Talk all of these things out so we can just go on.

I know, we've been so long together that we are inept.
I know, it's hard to trust,
but it's all that we've got left.
Time passes, we get lost and lonely, then reach for anything.
The questions all are academic
as love has nothing to bring.
I know we can go on this way of with and without,
but I know we can't continue with this shadow of a doubt.

22

It Ain't Going To Happen Tonight

The plans were made, the games were played, all obligations met.
The risks were weighed, the money paid,
and everything was set.
My ducks in a row, I'm ready to go, for the moment to come along.
But I sit instead, scratching my head
wondering what went wrong.
The timing was on, my problems were gone,
I did everything just right.
I covered each base, kept up with her pace,
but it ain't going to happen tonight.

Kids are away, the phone's on delay, I'm looking for place to land.
Lights are low, conversations' slow,
feels like it's going as planned.
It all binds and ties with that look in her eyes,
and I think things to be like they should.
but as I finally close in, she gets funny and grins
and I know things are not looking good.

I proceed in the groove, ready to make the move,
but she doesn't feel the time is right.
So I'm left high and dry, resolving with a sigh,
it ain't going to happen tonight.

The harder I try, to make everything right
the worse things get tangled and bound.
Though I don't understand why, I try and I try,
try to turn things around.

The plans were made, the games were played, all obligations met.
The risks were weighed, the money paid,
and everything was set.
My ducks in a row, I'm ready to go, for the moment to come along.
But I sit instead, scratching my head
wondering what went wrong.
Thoughtful and sure, resolved and secure,
I gracefully say, "It's all right".
And it's hard to hide how I feel now inside,
knowing, it ain't going to happen tonight.

23

I Am The Fool Who's In Charge Of It All

There is no hidden reasons for this sad falling away,
the fault is all mine. I take all the blame.
With nowhere else to go, nobody else to call,
I am the fool who's in charge of it all.

I shouldn't be surprised; she doesn't want me to return.
My bridges are still blazing from the fires I left burn.
I hurt her, she left me, now I'm stuck with my own gall,
and I am the fool who's in charge of it all.

I think how could she hurt me just because I am a lout,
but then again where was my head when I let that girl walk out?

With a pig head too thick, I wouldn't try to see her side,
I must have pushed her too far, always needing to be right.
Pretending I didn't need her, High and mighty, strong and tall,
now I am the fool who's in charge of it all.

I'd like her to know my changes since we've been apart,
but just saying I'm sorry won't heal a broken heart.

Still sulking from my wrong approach to this fight,
wondering if there's ever any way to make things right.
My mistakes and short-comings caused my whole world to fall,
I am the fool who's in charge of it all.

24

Somewhere In Between

Arguments won't solve the problems
and these feelings need to cease.
What we both want can't be met, but what we need is peace.
In your mind, you think you're right
while I want to follow my dream,
there must be a way we both can feel good somewhere in between.
All this distance separating us just proves the point that it should.
But Honey, it's not really doing either of us any good.
Seems to me it's a no-win game, that's all it's ever been.
Maybe a solution lies somewhere in between.
Our lines are drawn for battle though the area is mostly gray.
Is the risk of gaining vantage worth throwing everything away.
Should we continue with attitudes one-sided crass and mean?
Or, could we surrender and seek a truce somewhere in between.
You can close your mind and then your heart
while I sting my words at you.
but can't you see the end results is tearing us both in two.
I'd like to put this all behind us and start all over clean.
live within the compromise somewhere in between.

25

The Yodeler

My Daddy played accordion and sang his western songs,
all us kids would sing along, singing all the evening long.
Then Daddy would get loose, and yodeling would begin.
I felt kind of dumb within so I never quite joined in.

Through many years that passed a change came over me.
I started singing memories, but I sang them secretly.
Still embarrassed and unsure, I sang the nights alone.
Though I could move those "A"s and "O"s,
I never shared it with a soul.

Yodelayee, yodelayee, yodelayee who,
singing kie yie yippie yippie aye.
Yodelayee, yodelayee, yodelayee who,
singing kie yie yippie yippie aye.

Trying to meet their expectations,
torn between opposing poles.
I lost sight of my goals sang and acted out false roles.
Till one day I sang for pleasure, not to impress anyone.

The kids all joined in some, and we all had lots of fun.
As I strum guitar & yodel I think of Dad, Gene and Roy,
wondering if they too were coy
yodeling songs when they were boys.
I have learned that to be happy
I must judge things for myself,
don't just do for someone else, but do it for yourself.

Yodelayee, yodelayee, yodelayee who,
singing kie yie yippie yippie aye.
Yodelayee, yodelayee, yodelayee who,
singing kie yie yippie yippie aye.

26

Tumbleweed

See the birds winging over the bay,
I can't go, but you can't stay, my Love.
Winter winds are whispering your name,
you've no want to stay that game and follow.
So fly away, fly away my Love.

Long goodbyes, like the leaves turning brown,
too many words to explain the down
we're both feeling.
I can't stand to watch you die,
I know how these winters bring sorrow.
I can't cage the fire in your eyes,
as you gaze down that road for tomorrow.
So fly away, fly away my Love.

You're a tumbleweed, growing roots in the fall
to roll to the south as summer winds call you to roll.
Cars are calling from the highway of dreams,
your lifeblood is pulling you back in it's stream so go.
and fly away, fly away my Love.

27

MEMOIRS & NOTES - II - 'A LONG WAY FROM MY HOME'

A Long Way From My Home

(1978) – During the late summer of 1966, when I was 16, we lived in Southeast Portland, in an area called Westmoreland. At first, we lived in an apartment owned by Clarence, Grandma Scarbrough's boyfriend, who allowed us to stay there while mother got on her feet financially. That summer my mother could not find a job, but due to our circumstances, I qualified and went to work for the federal Job Corps program, working as a laborer on the park land situated in back of Portland's Washington Hills, cutting trails and creating forest paths, armed with pulaskis, shovels, picks and rakes. In the interim, mother moved us to a large three-story house with a full basement also in Westmoreland.

Mother's father, (Grandpa Scarbrough), got really sick. He was living on the east side of Mt. Hood in Redmond

Oregon. He had a bad case of emphysema from breathing and eating too much dirt and dust driving an open-cab road grader for 20 years; this, compounded by his smoking way too much. So, after hearing he was bedridden, mother and I drove over to Redmond, literally dragged him out of his sick bed in the Hotel Redmond and moved him into the big yellow house with us.

It was my job after I got home from working in the hills and later, after school started, when I came home from football practice, (Cleveland High School), to take care of Grandpa Scarbrough and to help Richie make dinner for the family.

It was during those many months of his convalescence that I got to know Grandpa Scarbrough,... and during those times, while I sat in the chair next to

Grandpa Scarbrough ca 1942

him as he lay in his bed coughing his brains out, in between breathing through his oxygen mask and taking drags off of his Chesterfields, he told a great deal about his life, his loves, his fears, his accomplishments, and even some of his failures. He had a love for Crown Royal and Seagram 7, and would have a bottle stashed in corners or under his pillow or mattress, or in a coat pocket in the closet. Mother would find these bottles and throw them away. It was my task, and later my duty, to find these bottles that had been relocated or thrown away, recollect them and restore them to their rightful owner. Grandpa, who always had more money than mother knew about, would pay me a quarter every time I recovered one of his treasured bottles. From those conversations and intimate moments, which burned into my thoughts, I grew to have a great appreciation for that man, regardless of his many faults.

And so, in 1978, ten years after his passing, I set out to try to document in words and this poem; the life and times of my grandpa, Ray E. Scarbrough. "**A Long Way From My Home**," documents his early life as a cowboy, as a hobo, as a lumberjack, as a Caterpillar road grader driver, his escapades as a bootlegger which led to some jail time, all the while reflecting on his strong desire to return to a life and place that had passed years earlier.

Side Note:

It was 1992, some time during the fall, I had heard about this contest that was being put on by a country and western radio station in Aberdeen, (Aberdeen, Washington). Of course, I was very excited, and I signed up for the occasion. On the day of the tryouts, I drove to Aberdeen and met the judges, and some of the other people trying out for this contest. A temporary stage had been set up outside and there were a lot of people standing around listening to the contestants. As we were standing around waiting for our turn to get up on the makeshift stage to do our thing, I noticed that most of the other C&W contestants came dressed for the part, with their cowboy hats and boots and cowboy shirts or blouses, and I, arriving after work, was under dressed and I felt I looked like one of the people in the audience waiting for the next act. I felt out of place, and the more I stood there, the more I just wanted to get in my car and drive home. The one thing there that excited me, and was ultimately the reason I stayed, was that there was a house band up there on the stage to help and backup the contestants if they so wanted. And me, with just an acoustic guitar and voice, I felt like it might give me a better chance. I vacillated on what song to do and in hindsight I guess now that I should have done "**You've Got To Believe**" but I chose this song instead, thinking it told a better story and had good lyrics.

By the time I got up on the stage I had listened to so many of the other performers and groups, many that had what I felt to be better material, that I knew I wasn't even in the running anymore. But here's the deal, I got up on the stage, went to the bass player who seemed to be in charge, gave him the chord progression to "A Long Way From My Home" and,... and it was awesome. Awesome to hear my material with a professional band backing me up. Awesome to have the attention of the audience, awesome that the band harmonized with me on the chorus. Everybody else was doing two- or three-minute songs and here I was with a six-minute song. I ended up doing four of the six verses which was still a lot longer than the others. When I finished the judges seemed to avoid eye contact and I knew then, when they said they'd call me, I knew then what the results were. But I did get to do one of my own songs with a band backing me up and, it was glorious. As I was getting off the stage, the keyboard player motioned for me to come over and he said, "That, my friend, was really a great song. I 'm sure I'm gonna hear from you again; uh, Lord Baldwin? Yeah," he said, looking around to the rest of the group that were nodding their heads in agreement, "Good job, Lord Baldwin." I drove home stoked, knowing I was as good as I had imagined myself to be.

A Shadow Of A Doubt

(1992) – My brother Ray remarried for the third time to a girl named Shauna. Many felt that their relationship was doomed from the start because Ray was old enough to be her father. Not only that, but Ray was just finishing up raising his first set of kids as his youngest, Randy, left home after high school. Still, the relationship seemed to flourish at times and they created a new family. She came into the marriage with a small baby boy and together they had four more children, one boy, Matthew in 88, and three girls, Melissa in 1990, Crystal in 1992 and Sarah in 1994. And things were wonderful for a while.

One day I went down there to visit and saw a side of Shauna that made me glad I was living 135 miles away. She had been over-critical of Ray and his work for that week, accusing him of hiding money. But the thing that really irked me was her insinuations that he was running around on her and seeing some other girls. I do know my brother has many faults and probably deserves the consequences he falls into, but I also felt that, like me, he had always taken his fidelity extremely seriously and would never do something like that. Later that year I was down again visiting and the subject was breeched again. This time, after we were alone, Ray confided with me that he thought maybe the reason she was accusing him of this heinous act was because she was guilty of it herself. Come to find out later on, she had been running around on him for some time, and at the time of their divorce, she was pregnant from some previous rendezvous.

Side Note:

This is another poem I wrote in 1991-1992, about realizing that there is always a need for reopening communication lines after a breach of trust. In between jamming with Ray Matthews and being unemployed for those many months. This was one that he really liked and later we did this one live on stage at the church, and we were well received. Ray Matthews and I talked about doing something more than what we were accomplishing and even talked about taking some of my material on the road, which sounded good at the time when I was unemployed but that quickly ended when I went back to work at the Parks dept.. Because this was a love song of sorts and had a nice up-tempo, it was a good song to do in public.

It Ain't Going To Happen Tonight

(1992) – Ever have one of those nights where you had big plans, you thought you were in control and you were sure nothing could go wrong? Ever have one of those plans that you can't see how it could possibly go bad but then you find out just how wrong you could be? This song was based on fact; the names have been changed to protect the innocent. Unfortunately this factor that we're dealing with can be formulated by multiplying however many ongoing problems you might have by the day of the week, like Monday to stay Wednesday and Thursday in the multiplying factor of 2, Friday, Saturday and Sunday in the multiplying factor of 5, and then, that figure times however many children you have and then, pick a number and divide that figure by the fickleness of the female gender and you have a formula that might give you some indication of your success/failure rate.

It was Friday, March 30th, 1990. We found out a month earlier that Diane was expecting Allison, (number eight). Also, on that Friday, March 30th, 1990, my job of 14 years ended when the JW Electronics Store went out of business, (maybe more on that, later). After finding out (that same day), that the new owners, Diane's sister Kathy and her husband Ron, did not want to keep me on to work at their newly formed company, Electronics Resources Inc., I was scrambling to get myself into a new career; something totally different than sales related, and I was in the process of enrolling in SPSCC to start college, which was due at begin the following Monday, April 2nd. Are you feeling the pressure yet? Most of all though. we were going to be celebrating Diane's 40th birthday, which was two days earlier on Wednesday the 28th.

So, we had this evening where we were going out to dinner and then to a movie, (don't tell the kids, but we were going to get a sneak peek at the, *"Teenage Mutant Ninja Turtles"* movie that had come out that very day, on March 30th), and then we were going to come home and hopefully we might spend some needed, quality time together.

Lori, who was 16, was going over to her friend Sarah's house, and Chet, who was 14 was going over to Aaron's house, but we had two of the girls, Elizabeth, 12, and Meridith, 10, staying home that night to be babysitters, for Ben who was 8, Stephen who was 6, Spencer who was 4, and Christopher who was almost two. The vehicle, a 1970s Dodge Sportsman extended van was working fairly favorably, and unusually, we had our itinerary set pretty well.

A complete chicken, potatoes, and vegetables dinner was in the oven; Diane had just gotten out of a shower and was getting dressed while I put together food on plates on the table.

The first problem occurred when I realized that someone had either forgotten to turn the oven on or one of the kids accidentally turned the oven off; okay, we go to plan "B" and I grabbed eggs, some Bacon, threw a few potatoes into the microwave and began looking for bread to make some toast.

And now Christopher starts crying and wants to nurse, and Spencer is bouncing off the walls wanting something to eat right now. Diane, who is smelling great and has a wonderful red dress, on, goes into the bedroom and pacifies Christopher while I realize there is no bread. I ask Meridith to watch the potatoes while I go to the little grocery store, a few blocks down the street, and get some bread. Meanwhile time is passing and by the time I get back to the house with the bread we have missed our window of opportunity to get to the movie at the early showing. Ben and Stephen are arguing in the back room over the game in the floppy disk drive in the Atari 800 computer, and Elizabeth is yelling at both of them to stop fighting. Although Meridith is assigned the task of watching the potatoes, she forgets and one side of them is very dark and crispy, (burnt). I try to coordinate the cooking of the eggs and the toast and I lineup a bunch of bowls and start filling them up with this makeshift breakfast/dinner and yell for everyone to get to the table.

Diane asks for a few more minutes and then Christopher is asleep. After Diane puts herself back together again, we give instructions to the kids and head out the front door. And now our time has shrunk considerably, but I figure the evening is not totally wasted; we can go out and have a sundae or something and still spend some time together afterwards.

I haven't driven five miles before Diane is worried about something dealing with the kids; moreover, I'm there wondering if I had shut everything off on the stove after I finished making dinner. We make a decision to go back for just a second. This was the biggest mistake of the evening because when we entered those doors, we were in fact, admitting that we belonged to them. Oh, we did try to get away again, but Christopher woke back up again and Diane decided it would be best to nurse him again. So now it's ten o'clock as we leave the house a second time and start driving towards town. how hard it is to put romance together after dealing with a large family and an unpredictable, equivocal wife? Don't try to answer this. We didn't make it very far before Diane says, "I don't really feel like going out anymore."

"Okay so now what?" I think, and slowdown. We sit there at the crossroads trying to decide whether we should go forward into the night to salvage the romantic date or turn around and go back home and try to grasp something else of what's left of the evening. By this time, I don't really feel like going out anymore either, so as she decides for us to go back home, although I still want to get romantically involved, my drive and desires are slowly fading away.

We no sooner get into the house and the children detain us, who, because it's the weekend, want a, "something-special treat." Diane gives me that look, that special look at says, "wait till later and we'll spend some time together." So, we pacify the kids and start to settle them into their beds, but Christopher is upset and wants to nurse, yet again. So, Diane put on her nightclothes, grabs Christopher, goes into the living room, sitting in her rocking chair, and nurses Christopher while watching TV. I grab my guitar and go down the hallway, between the kid's rooms, and sing some songs hoping to put them all to sleep. My mission seemingly accomplished, I go back into the living room and Diane is fast asleep with Christopher still plugged in. I wake her up and point her towards the bedroom, only to realize that, "***It Ain't Gonna Happen Tonight.***"

I Am The Fool Who's In Charge Of It All

(1985) – This poem was written in my comeback days at the funeral home. Like "Blue With A Broken Heart," and Meridith decided this was a good song, and after learning the words, insisted on singing it whenever we had company over. It became a favorite of mine after I realized how well received it was as I played it for family, friends and company that came over. After finalizing the funeral arrangements for a 40-year-old man that accidentally died in his bathtub, his mother, who was in her late 60s, asked me to come over to her place to sign the paperwork. When I got there she had a bunch of his stuff in the living room and asked me to take what I wanted and give the rest to Goodwill. There was a trumpet and a cheap guitar that I thought might be good to give to the kids. (This trumpet, that we still have, was used in school by Chet, Lori, Ben, Stephen, Spencer and now Allison). I took the guitar to work and hid it behind one of the caskets in the display room. Although it was beat up and the frets were a bit off, I was in this creative period and sometimes inspiration needed me to do things then and there. I was strumming these blues chords when the song popped out at me. This guy comes to the realization that all the problems of his failed relationship and the love-gone-wrong scenarios fall back on him and reflect his attitudes and poor decisions that leads him to the realization that, as he admits to himself, *"I Am The Fool Who's In Charge Of It All."*

Side Note:

As was my hope from the beginning, I felt that if I couldn't make it as a performer doing my own material, maybe I could get someone else to do my material and help me push forward in my songwriting career. As you may have read before, I was always about getting my song out there, writing for, *Elvis, Johnny Cash, James Taylor, Waylon Jennings, Marie Osmond, Willie Nelson, Dolly Parsons,* and a host of others. This song, which was originally inspired by and written for *Merle Haggard,* became an instant hit with my friends and family, especially my daughter Meridith, who at the time, was about 5 or 6, and who somehow remembered the words to the poem, and sang the song all the time.

Another Side Note:

This song has be rerecorded a few times, each time with the hope that I might get a bit closer to the inspirational piece of *Meryl Haggard's* that I was emulating; "*Misery & Gin.*" But I never could because they're two different songs with different meters and messages. It's okay though, putting my talent next to *Meryl's* is kind of a compliment in itself, isn't it? Or reality check; I was nowhere close,...

Somewhere In Between

(1985) – This poem was also written in my comeback days at the funeral home. After working at the funeral home for a while and interacting with the managing Funeral Director, Gary Rook, I started to understand what it was I was doing, as a Licensed Funeral Director and Embalmer, (working off of Gary's licenses), and in the process, I started to believe in my abilities and myself. Also, because I was exposed to Mr. Rook's extensive vocabulary, my own vocabulary increased.

This whole experience opened up new channels and suddenly my songwriting block was over. I experimented with a lot subjects and ideas and was writing lyrics about everything that sounded good. This poem is about someone trying to look at some problem or argument from both sides; the give and take, the cooperation, negotiation, compromise and hopefully, the reconciliation.

I drove to work angry one morning, after an argument with Diane. During a cooling down period at work, I analyzed the incidence and wrote down my feelings and observations of the occurrence. In between funeral services, my voice echoed through empty funeral home chapel as I composed the music on the organ in there. That night when I got home, in hopes of getting back on the better side of my relationship, I played the song for Diane, and knew it right away that it was a good song, especially after she started crying, and except for the kids, Diane's response was the one and only gauge I had to work with,...

Side Note:

funny thing, though I thought I had a hit with this song and that I would later rerecord the song later on, I never did. The thing to know is, after Chris's passing, and me getting entrenched in my musical work, I was suddenly barraged with more material than I could possibly record. And that, along with the fact that I still had loads of material still waiting for me to give attention to, maybe not surprising that I did not get back to this song.

The Yodeler

(1991) – I always wanted to be a yodeler, you know, a cowboy singing on the prairie, yodeling and slurring his words out there by a campfire, and topped off with a rousing harmonica finale. When I was younger and living in Grandma Scarbrough's house, we would go to these special events called Swing Fests, which was a Swiss spring celebration. Richie and I, who were not Swiss, wore these little Swiss kippahs (yarmulkes) and black vests that had little decals and flags, and we walked around the whole area picking up beer bottles, which we got one penny apiece for, and converted them into cash. Even though we were the only ones doing this, there was a lot of people drinking beer and so there was good money to be made. In the evenings, there would be lots of sausages, salads, breads, and desserts, including these thin, Eucharist-like fine wafers that tasted a lot like the waffle-wafer ice cream cones. Anyway, in the evenings the music would strike up, people would get excited, accordions would be playing,

people would be eating sausages, drinking more beer, dancing the polka, and as the music went on into the night, a whole lot of yodeling would loudly and unashamedly emerge.

A lot of times I would tolerate going to the swing fests only for the evenings with the dancing, the pretty young girls, those wonderful Swiss candy bars, the wonderful music, and the yodeling. Sometimes multiple people, men and women, would yodel in harmony and counterpoint and was just fascinating.

Side Note:

This poem is also a shout out to my dad, who plays excellent accordion and was a mighty good yodeler to boot. As the poem relates, I was a bit embarrassed to display my meager attempts at yodeling, but my dad did not judge, but instead, encouraged me, (and Richie) to join in when we felt like it. I remember him suppressing a smile when I did such a poor job of yodeling to one of my dad's favorite accordion tunes, "The Beer Barrel Polka."

Tumbleweed

(1969) – As maybe mentioned in "Something Must Be Wrong," this poem was originally conceived and worked with in the winter of 1968 on a friend's piano in Brown's Mills, New Jersey. During the summer of 1968 while working at the Concord hotel in upstate New York, and later on, while I was going to school, every weekend, it was my pleasure and self-assigned duty to roam the small cocktail lounges and mini-bars that were located all over the Concord Hotel, and play on/with one of the many baby-grand pianos in that hotel, of which, there was no shortage.

I would find a way to get into the hotel, usually through the back, service door entrance past the security guards, then I'd find one of those places with an open piano and start playing. The pianos were always located in some dark corner, which helped me maintain my anonymity while allowing me to try out some of my new material. My slight, but enthusiastic repertoire was usually well received by any who might be listening. I knew that realistically, my mostly drunken audience was not picky about what was being played, but it felt good to have people clap after a song and even drop a dollar or change of any denomination into the empty glass that I had conveniently but strategically placed on the top of the piano.

This song was originally played without words. Many of the bartenders got to know me and some of them liked what I did. I wasn't that good, but when you're playing in a dimly lit room to a bunch of people that were getting tight, people that would thrive on emotional music, (which just happens to be my type of music), things had a way of working out. Again, as I mentioned before, I was even asked more than once by different hotel Recreational Coordinators, if I wanted a job playing piano for the guests. I was shy and told him that I only did my own material and then they would smile and say, "Maybe later," but who knows what might have happened if in fact I would quit my job is a busboy and went to work in the hotel?

The second half of my senior year was spent in a small high school out in Donald, Oregon, called, North Marion High School. Because I had moved around so much and attended so many different schools, my transcripts were all screwed up. When I arrived, I was informed that I had too many years of PE and not enough math. So I had to double up on math classes and I had two days a week where I had an hour to do nothing. I arranged with the choir teacher to be let into the music room so I could play around on the piano. It was during one of those hours that I finally composed the words to this poem and put them to the music for this song about how he/she loves him/her and sees the possibilities of a relationship but knows that the other doesn't want that type of relationship; moreover he/she decides that if they are to be truly happy, they must let the other go.

28

12 - YOU'VE GOT TO BELIEVE - 1992

29

NOTES ABOUT THE COVERS

Okay, I have to admit that when I first created the cover for this album, "You've Got To Believe" I must have been in a big hurry because now, as much as then, I never liked it. I mean, sure, it was whimsical in its own way, with a lot of things going on, but unbelievable? I don't think so. The back cover with its flying saucer hovering over a house was a bit more unbelievable or at least, provocative than the front.

Frankly, I found this JPG while looking for something else. I loved the color in it and I just kept it. 'You've Got To Believe,' right?

Also, this was pre-CD days and the black and white, 1 ½ inch square in a cassette case wouldn't have done anything for you anyway.

30

YOU'VE GOT TO BELIEVE

You've Got To Believe
A Face Among Faces
I'm Going On
Not So Fast
He Doesn't Stay Home Anymore
A Dreamer
You're So Smart
When You Touch My Heart

"You've Got To Believe," Copyright © - October of 1992,
All Rights Reserved

31

You've Got To Believe

I believe we can do anything we set our minds to,
doesn't matter what we did or where we've been.
Times are hard now, but we'll make it somehow
and rise to the occasion again.
You see all these barriers, you feel out of touch,
and so overwhelmed, like it's all too much.

Don't give up, when it's a heavy load,
things are bound to get harder
as we head on down the road.
But Baby, don't give up on this dream of you and me,
if you want this love to work,
Babe, you've got to believe.

I believe in you, and all the things that you can do,
your goodness is just so hard to find.
You see everyone else, and you're too hard on yourself.
You feel you've fallen somehow behind.
This life is hard, dreams get put on delay,
I know at times you feel like driving away.

But don't give up, when it's a heavy load,
things are bound to get harder
as we head on down the road.
Oh Baby now, don't give up on this dream of you and me,
if you want this love to work,
Babe, you've got to believe.

I know about the trials a new love can bring,
but together, you and I, can do anything.

So don't give up, when it's a heavy load,
things are bound to get harder
as we head on down the road.
Baby, don't give up on this dream of you and me,
if you want this love to work,
Babe, you've got to believe.

32

A Face Among Faces

She smiled in passing and walked on her way,
to the work or appointments, she met every day.
I thought I might try to approach her, but doubt,
and the courage, the words never seemed to come out.
Still, each day she passed in the morning and night,
till I found myself waiting to see her go by.
No idea where she came from or where she might go,
I just knew a face and a voice of hello.

A face among faces, a face in the crowds,
hiding her life there, behind her facial shrouds.
Still people behind faces all have the need,
to call in soft silence,
"Please notice me."

Was she searching for meaning while walking the street,
when I'd just get a nod from our daily meet?
Was she waiting for me to approach her and ask?
I could hardly know much from the smiles of her mask.
Then one day she didn't pass, and life still went on,

but I was so empty from her being gone.
I resolved when I next gazed on her face again,
I'd let her know how I felt about her then.

A face among faces, a face in the crowds,
hiding the anguish behind facial shrouds.
All the people behind faces still have their needs,
and call in desperate silence,
"Please notice me."

She'd had fallen into sadness and taken her life.
All the passions of her face went with her that night.
It's too late for reasons, for fault or for blame.
Sad, I knew her by sight, but I never knew her name.

She was a face among faces, a face in the crowds,
hiding the anguish behind facial shrouds.
All the people behind faces still have their needs,
and call in desperate silence,
"Please notice me."

33

I'm Going On

I'm going on, to follow feelings of the heart.
Beyond this freeze, past empty trees
on the path that twists and bends.
I'm going on, I feel it's time for me to start.
I have this need to go to see where the road ends.

I'm going on, I know you can't go with me now.
But you'll endure and you're secure with all your many friends.
I'm going on, to greener pastures in the south.
I need to find if peace of mind is where the road ends.

I'm going on, continuing where I left off.
I live this way, day to day with no compromise or amends.
I'm going on, where sunny skies never stop.
I won't look back but make new tracks to where the road ends.

I'm going on, to fill desires long denied
If the world is round, I may be found back here someday again.
I'm going on, to find the person deep inside.
Maybe we'll meet there on the streets where the roads end.

34

Not So Fast

Everything I thought love should be
is coming together for you and me.
Most of my fears and concerns just fall away as our time turns.
Yet this urgency seems to persist,
like you're trying to follow some list.
I don't want to cramp your style,
but you need cool your jets for a while.

Not so fast, slow down and allow things to flow.
Love will last if we make time to let things grow.
You're in some kind of hurry that kind of makes me worry
this relationship might not last.
Take your time, let's fall in love, but not so fast.

Everything I hoped we could be
is coming true like some wonderful dream.
We have so much coming through,
and we have so much to look forward to.
Yet at times we seem out of place,
like we're running and losing some race.

I'm in no hurry for a broken heart,
or a relationship that's falling apart.

Not so fast, slow down and allow things to flow.
Love will last if we make time to let things grow.
You're in some kind of hurry that kind of makes me worry,
this relationship might not last.
Take your time, let's fall in love but not so fast.

35

He Doesn't Stay Home
Anymore

He stays at work till after ten,
goes home to the, "Where have you been?"
Gets in a fight over something way back when
and goes to bed, alone again.
He thinks of all the things he's tried to avoid the forces to collide.
He thinks of love that all but died, he even thinks of suicide.
He wonders what he stays there for,
he doesn't stay home anymore.

He talks to her without any gain,
speaks to the children on some other plane.
Acts out the part and hides the pain
and no one sees them going down the drain.
She's given up on her fine gift,
it's his damn fault that things have turned like this.
She thinks with time things just might shift,
but it won't be her that breaks the rift,
besides, all's fair in love and war,

and he doesn't stay home anymore.

He knows the chances are mighty slim
for her to ever succumb to him.
He Knows his future is sad and grim,
if they never talk beyond vague or dim.
He sees his life with nothing to hold,
as the same sad story, already told.
He sees a relationship, tired and old,
and without love he is empty and cold.
With no hope of change, just this in store,
he doesn't stay home anymore.

36

A Dreamer

I think someday I'll be somewhere,
comfortably relaxed in an easy chair.
Sing myself my songs in the dew of dawn,
but all you pessimists keep walking on my lawn
saying I'm a dreamer, a dreamer. and I'll die in my own frustration
if I never come to your realization.
But you live your life the way that you choose,
I'll live life my way, do the things I want to do.

I think someday we'll all be free;
with love and hope I know it could be.
Working together, through just laws,
but all you're looking for is flaws,
and I'm a dreamer, a dreamer;
You say the only peace is your own peace of mind,
but if you seek no beauty you must truly be blind.
The love waits to grow within the pit of your greed
but without care and compassion, it'll always be a seed.

37

You're So Smart

You're so smart; you finally got things to go your way.
Didn't give her room for a single word to say.
You directed it all like some dramatic play.
Orchestrated to such a fine art, you're so smart.

You're so smart; you made her take the heavy part of a fool.
Twisting words around and changing all the rules.
Standing your ground, acting so cool.
She was so helpless as you tore her all apart,
you're so smart.

You're so wise,... to think that she believed in all your lies.
You're so right; that's why you sit alone here tonight.

You're so smart to give the silent treatment to your best friend,
to make it too hard for her to make amends.
You got the house all to yourself again.
And it was so easy for you to break her heart,
you're so smart.

38

When You Touch My Heart

So much to say, so much to relate, so little time.
We all fight the same disease of loneliness inside.
We're all on this great big planet millions of people there
trying to touch a heart to show all that they care.
The moment is special, as charity overcomes the strife.
Unselfish persons reaching out to share their lives.
Sorrow is gone, instead, hope for the day to share,
when you touch my heart to show me that you care.
Skies grow dark, foreboding; rain falls when should be fair.
People, apprehensive run for shelter everywhere.
And still you reach out, to untangle me in my snare,
when you touch my heart to show me that you care.
Sometimes the risk is great, sometimes the faith is gone,
and its hard to know the right directions to go on.
But you take the wild chances, willing to take the dare,
when you touch my heart to show me that you care.
So much to say, so much to relate, and there is just so little time.
We all share the same disease of loneliness inside.
You know the cure, my love, you know it's always there,
when you touch my heart to show me that you care.

39

MEMOIRS & NOTES - 12 - 'YOU'VE GOT TO BELIEVE'

You've Got To Believe

(1992) – In Lori's junior and senior year, she decided that she really liked country western music and it was on in her bedroom, and in the living room, all the time. When we traveled anywhere in the car, she vacillated between her pop music and her country & western. After she graduated from Tumwater High School in 1992, she was ready to go to college and, in our 1970s Dodge extended van, we drove her up to Western Washington University which is located in Bellingham. This was in fact, a three-hour trip up and three-hour trip back, and we, (did I mention we took the whole family with us?), had the pleasure of listening to Lori's country and western music all the way up there.

As I drove, I listened to and tried to analyze all the words to the songs that were being played on the radio. Somewhere between Tacoma and Federal Way I started jotting down notes and some make shift lyrics. I turned the radio down and handed Lori a pencil and paper and started dictating most of the words of this poem, to her. By the time we reached Bellingham, I had most of the makings for this song along with two others. When I got home that night, I sat down with my guitar

117

and finished combining the lyrics and the music together which had been sitting in my head waiting to get out. This song was the first and perhaps the best of the three songs that I wrote from that trip.

At the time I thought that maybe somebody like Eddie Rabbit might do this song, but after he died May 8, 1998 of lung cancer I kind of gave up on that idea. But, don't give up when things get hard and times get hard, and leaning on someone can be good for both the leaner and the lean-ee. After recording this song, I felt that I came close to what I was looking for with this song. Even now, I still enjoy doing it myself, and performed it onstage at the stake center at an evening devoted to country and western music. Unfortunately, I couldn't hear the backup part of the tune being played to help me stay in sync and the results were that I was a little bit more than a little off, but most of the crowd was forgiving and I did an encore song afterwards that, because I played live, was better than the first.

Side Note:

In a way, this poem speaks to me like it is the embodiment of all of my works; poetry, musical compositions, other writings; speaking collectively to me. Telling me that they believe in me and the things that I can do, they know that I see the world of music, they know that I compare myself with the successful others and that I feel inadequate, but they admonish me, while saying, "Hey there, Lord Baldwin, don't give up when it's a heavy load," and remind me, in a positive way, saying, "if you want this thing to work, Baby, *you've* got to believe." And so, being advised by my own poetic works, how could I not feel the importance of the work I do? But, kind of funny, looking at it that way, right?

Another Side Note:

My nephew Randy loved to hear me sing this song, especially close to the end of the song in the chorus as my voice got a little weird. In fact, I was jamming one time with Randy's brother, Phillip, over at his basement studio, and Randy asked if we could do this song. Even though I didn't have any crib sheets and I had to teach a chord progression to a couple of other guys that didn't even know me, we had great session and Randy appeared to have a good time, being sure to shout out the,.. "Babe ee."

A Face Among Faces

(**1991**) – During the summer of 1966, I got up at 5:30 every morning to catch one of the government buses that came around and picked up the Job Corp people to take them to work, up into the back of the Washington Hills in a large Northwestern wooded area of Portland.

We lived in Westmoreland so I had to walk about 15 blocks down SE Milwaukee Avenue to catch the Job Corp Crew Bus. Along the way I would meet up with a friend, another guy my age named Andy. Together we would walk the rest of the way down SE Milwaukee Avenue to catch the Job Corp Crew Bus at Powell Street before the bus took us across the Ross Island Bridge and onward to our work site. Most everyday, when we got to the bus stop, there would almost always be this same well-dressed girl waiting there for a city bus. She was, from appearances and mannerisms, probably 18 or 19. Being 16, I felt an enmity as big as that Ross Island Bridge that spanned the eastern and western shores of the Willamette River.

After a short while, we did talk to each other, but there was usually less than five minutes from the time she got there and her bus arrived, and she wasn't there every day, so we never had much of a close relationship. My conversations with her were just superficial and always in passing, and never with any depth, but as the summer went on, I grew to look forward to our semi-daily get-together.

Everyone has a tale about procrastination and one of mine came one day, nearing the end of August. It was close to the time our work period would be completed with the government and the other teenagers still in school, like Andy and I, would soon be returning to school. Even though I was extremely shy, I thought I might get to know her better, find out where she lived, and maybe get her number, and maybe take her out to a movie or something. After all, recognizing, understanding or maybe realizing the importance of each and every one of us is important. Anyway, I had resolved one Sunday night, close to two weeks before our work would end, that I would be bold and brave and set something up. This was going to be a bit difficult because I knew she was a couple years older than I was, but I felt that the worse that could happen was that she would just no, and, because it was close to the end of the season for us to work, I would be going back to school and wouldn't have to face her and my rejection for more than a week or so.

But although I got there early and waited there with Andy, who knew of my plan and was snickering with speculation over my probable outcome, she didn't come that Monday. In fact, she stopped coming to the bus stop altogether for that whole week. Andy and I continued to look for her to return, but she never did. Andy and I made it to the bus stop early every day of that next week, but sadly,

she didn't come then either. I soon started school, and after awhile I completely forgot about her.

One day I went over to Andy's house to play a game of chess with him. He met me at the door, excited, with the newspaper in his hand and turned to one of the inside pages and pointed to the newspaper where there was a picture of what appeared to be this same girl. "That's her." Andy said excitedly. "I don't know." I replied with uncertainty. The article mentioned that it she lived in our area of town and that it was believed that she had committed suicide. To this day I don't know for sure if it was the same girl, maybe I should say, I hope not, but for years afterwards, I have wondered, "what if," like, what if it was the same girl, what if I'd struck up a conversation with her, what if her loneliness could have changed the outcome? I also know that some things need to be let go and ultimately, there was really nothing I could've done.

Side Note:

From reading this story, it should be obvious to you that I wrote the words to this poem from all that had happened, drawn from my recollections of that time and place at the bus stop on Powell Street and Milwaukee Avenue.

Another Side Note:

There were times, not many, but there were times when I would take the longer way home from Cleveland High School just to walk up Powell street to go by that bus stop; lust to remember, but because it was faster to get home cutting through the golf course, and because I needed to get home to take care of my grandpa, those longer trips diminished till I no longer went that way.

I'm Going On

(1991) – My time taking care of Grandpa Scarbrough left quite an impression on me. He told me many things

about his life, leaving nothing to the imagination, and I grew to know him better than I knew any male relative, including my own father. Although Grandpa Ray Scarbrough passed away in 1968, his stories, tales and escapades with their detailed descriptions of people, places, and the things, as well as his own attitudes and feel-ings that he had had back then; those thoughts and feelings have stayed with me ever since.

I was particularly impressed with his life and times as a rambler, which is not to be confused with the unsettling life of a bum, which in my opinion usually described a person that, for whatever reason, had given up, lacked a sense of purpose, positive motivation or even lost their passion with life itself, choosing instead to spend a portion of their lives in an unproductive manner, avoiding and despising work, and sometimes for an alcoholic, ending up in an alley or on Third and Burnside in a drunken stupor. I don't even think he was a hobo, (which he professed to be), because from my perspective back then, hobos were usually transients that for whatever reasons did not choose to stay in one place, for whatever reasons, vagrants, antisocial outcasts from society, who knows? From today's standards, anybody that is homeless could be defined as such.

What I know is that Grandpa Scarbrough was searching for himself and a purpose in life, drifting from town to town. He would stop in small towns and work there, trying to see if it was something he liked to do. Much of the time you would find him using any available railroad as part of his transportation from place to place, but he also hitchhiked to get to around.

After he left the reservation, and before he married Grandma Scarbrough in 1922, he tried on many hats to see which fit best. But his attitude usually ended up with him getting disillusioned with what it was he was doing at the time and then, after he felt he had stayed in one place too long, he would be finding himself "Going On," following the dream that motivates the heart all the way to the end of the road,... and beyond.

Not So Fast

(1992) – This was one of the other poems that I wrote from the trip to Western Washington University in Bellingham Washington. Right after I wrote the lyrics, because of the fact that this subject deals with taking time with their relationships; it was supposed, even by Diane, that this was one of those poems that I was writing, but had in mind that a woman would sing this song. Actually, the concept of, "Not So Fast," ultimately meant, let's give our relationship a little more time before we rush into something that we might regret later. This meaning—kind of like "let's slow down so we can cherish this newfound relationship," and was written without a gendered consideration, but I wouldn't mind is someone like Dolly Parton sang it. I'm sure she'd do a better job with it than me."

He Doesn't Stay Home Anymore

(1992) – After I started working at the college my duties were divided between me working for the Education Training Program that taught state employees a one-day crash course in computer sciences, and working in the AutoCAD lab, configuring computers, and helping students with their CAD homework. One day while working in the AutoCAD lab, I met a man that seemed to be extremely committed to his schooling. He stayed long hours during the open labs to get his homework done, but I even found him there late in the evenings and all day on Saturdays. One day I came up to speak to him in passing and I said to him in a joking manner, "I bet your family misses you."

He confessed, "I don't stay home anymore." Confused, I pressed for an explanation and found out that he was going through marital problems. He told me later about his fragile relationship with his wife of 15 years, his lack of communication with his children, and his un-happiness of life in general. He told me that after many months of living in this silent or antagonistic lifestyle, he had even considered suicide because things were so bad in his life. My obvious question to him was, "why don't you just leave?" He then told me that he wanted to try to make the whole thing work again, but he wasn't sure how he was going to have that happen, especially because he knew that his wife believed that he was running around on her. With this breakdown of communications and an acceptance of the sad circumstances by both parties, you can imagine, this didn't do too much for his relationship. But perhaps the worst part of their union was that even when he was home, he didn't relate to his wife or children. And so it was that he preferred to stay at school and do his homework instead of facing his problem at home and in doing so, he didn't stay home anymore but missed out on putting his family back together again.

Side Note:

Long after I finished writing this poem about him and his circum-stances, this same guy, we'll call him Robert, moved out of his home and out of the lives of his family and into an apartment in Olympia. This lasted for less than a month before he and his wife realized the folly of their ways and decided to get back together. The last I heard, Robert, his wife, and his kids were all going to therapy to try to put their lives and their family back together again.

A Dreamer

(1971) – This is another one of those poems that was written in my early guitar days, in 1971, when I was very hippy-opinionated, hoping for a better world. There was a lot of pessimistic and narrow-minded individuals running the country at the time, (Richard Nixon, Spiro Agnew) and influencing or indoctrinating perspectives to most of us in the younger set, not to mention the Robert McNamara war, oh, that is to say, the Vietnam war. I was willing to do my part to bring about a change, but in 1971 I was still trying to figure out who I was, and who was I to say how and what things could or should be, and how could we all bond or work together to affect the revolution without a good leader? And I was, well, kind of nobody; meanwhile, with the democrats blaming the failed world politics on the republican and the republicans blaming county's social and political unrest issues on the democrats as the United States as well as the world itself was going to hades in a hand basket.

Side Note:

The words to this poem combines my hopes of being left to my own designs in my nonconformist ways using my free agency and my own ideas, along with my hopes of finding peace in the hearts of rednecks and ultimately in hopes of ending the Vietnam War.

You're so Smart

(1991) – Imagine that there is this man that is sitting alone in a deserted living room trying to retrace the exquisite, but cutting and destructive behavior he just exhibited, while he can hear the faint sounds of his best friend and lover crying in another room. I got into an argument with Diane about who knows what and after I drove my point home leaving her no room for compromise or posturing, she left the room with the resulting statement, "you're so smart." I realized that my winning had caused a bifurcation in our relationship resulting in me seemingly winning the argument, but actually losing the battle. Having the last word can be satisfying for a fleeting moment, but the consequence of that cold and cruel outcome was not to my liking nor my desired results.

Side Note:

After coming to my senses and after making up with Diane, offering an apology for my hardheadedness, I wrote this poem to document and maybe sarcastically point out the dichotomy of the winning vs the losing stratagems to this potentially dangerous activity.

When You Touch My Heart

(1991) – Realizing that love; that true special love, can be motivated and obtained with the simplest of kind acts by just showing that you care. I was in the State Parks lunchroom one day talking to some of the other women workers. The subject of single parenting and their needs came up and the talk went on and on focusing on their (the single women's) problems dating and relationships, and, trying to include myself in the conversation, I said from out of the blue, "We all share the same disease of loneliness inside." From this one statement, which I wrote down on a napkin, a poem was born. I stayed up late after work that night and put the lyrics together, adding, "When you touch my heart" to the chorus line. At the time I had this other guitar tune that I was messing around with, so I just put these new words with that old tune and there you have it—it worked out wonderfully. Sometimes the marriage of words and music are so exquisite that I marvel at how it happened. This was one of those fusions—and again, one of the songs that didn't quite make it to the first two albums and then was shuffled around for a while till this album came out.

Side Note:

After I recorded this song, I brought my guitar to work and played this song for all the people that I could find that were in that earlier conversation. Needless to say, the song was well received.

Another Side Note:

By the way, it may have occurred to you that I have mentioned many times of interactions with different women that I came in contact with at the Washington State Parks Department, and frankly, it was the first time I had ever come in contact with multiple offices full of working women, most of which in need of technical support with their computers or the network, but also, some of them with their own sets of problems outside the office. And I would admit that it may seem odd, but I was always up front with them, and,... I don't know, Diane seems to think that I have this certain face and easy demeanor that lets others, including women, feel comfortable to talk with, to confide in and even comfortable enough to take council from. And I took it to heart that they all seemed to care about me as a person too. They loved it when Diane came in with our baby, Christopher, or when Lori would come in to use my computer and/or borrow the keys to my 67 Chevy Nova, and they loved me telling the stories of simple family catastrophes and triumphs, and I made a lot of good, true friends, some of which I met up with as they were coming and going at the college, either to take classes or to work for the different departments at the college itself.

SPECIAL NOTE

SPECIAL NOTE

In 1992, with the likes of, Mary Chapin Carpenter, Vince Gill, Garth Brooks, Anne Murray, Alabama, The Judds, Randy Travis, Clint Black, and George Strait, Country and Western music had reached a new audience and I wanted to get into the flow with those people. This here album, **"You've Got To Believe,"** as well as the album, **"A Long Way From My Home,"** and most of the songs therein, were, as maybe mentioned before, conceived and developed to be part of my new C&W concept albums. And after the songs were recorded and then engineered into these two entities, it felt good, not only to my ego that I could create these songs to accomplish my goal to compete in this market, but to then add them to my ten other albums; I was highly hopeful that if I could not break into the market myself, well, maybe one of my songs would. And after a while it seemed to me that some of the songs in the, **"You've Got To Believe"** album and most of the songs from the, **"A Long Way From My Home"** album, transcended beyond the C&W genre. Still, I put together a 60-minute cassette tape taking selections from both albums, called, **"Night Lights In The Country Skies"** and set them to wherever it looked like it might be noticed and hopefully, played. This was 1992 and there was a lot of avenues that could be taken, like C&W radio stations, that at that time and era, would sometimes play amateur recordings, and then there was the record companies that specialized in C&W formats. I even bought these special cardboard mailing sleeves designed for cassettes and put them inside a small manila envelope with a small business card with simple check boxes to help them report what they felt about the tape, and I included a second self-addressed, stamped envelope for them to mail back to me. Also, I put a hidden small piece of tape on the corner of the cassette box to reveal to me if someone had opened the box. Lots of effort and time and money we didn't have to go into this undertaking, all for, I don't know, I must have mailed out dozens of these demos and I guess I should have been happy that maybe three of them did come back to me; none of them had that secret tape breeched and none of them had any of the boxes checked. Very discouraging, but a bump in the road and a reminder that maybe I was, *'Just Not Good Enough"* at the time, but I did get better and I continued waltzing into country and western music,... not like what's out now, and I do wish I had some of their voices, but old country, like, sitting on the front porch and on a breezy summer night,... playing your guitar to the records and trying to figure out the chords and struggling to keep up,... but I was always looking to get better,...   I was in my twenties and highly influenced by what was on the radio,... and my brother Charlie who was race car crazy and he was silly with Country music,... and it was Charlie what turned me on to what was happening,... my favorite was and still is *'Wanted - The Outlaws'* what a phenomenal album,... it was a sound I wanted to make,... maybe with a bit of, 'the Band' music,... and there might need to be a harmonica,... and about tomorrow,... We'll see what's waiting for us tomorrow,... and thank you, Charlie,...

Side Note:

In a real way, because of my influences,... I was a part of that Old Country music happening in 1992 and some of my influenced songs were inspired by all of the artists in that era,... and I feel a sense of pride to be secretly, (invisibly), connected,... I'm not saying I'm in their league, far from it, but I continue to be moved,,,

41

❧

13 - A FAMILY MAN - 1992

42

NOTES ABOUT THE COVERS

Here again we have the original album cover. I liked the weird font on the cover so much that I used it for the poetry this 13 chapter. Judging from the ages of Lori, Chet and Liz, I put this photo to be taken around 1979.

I looked all around in 1992 to get something cool, but all my other photos looked so staged or Olan-Mills portrait-like and I didn't want that.

So here, arguably still staged, but you see the essence of a young man and his lovely wife, kind of kneeling behind a red wagon filled with their kids; the smile on the young man's face reflecting who and what he was, and still is, a devoted family man.

Names and ages from left to right: Lori...18, Spencer...6, Chet...16, Liz...14, Meridith...13, Stephen...8, Me...? Allison...almost 2, Diane...? and Benjamin...10-11.

43

A FAMILY MAN

A Family Man
It All Comes Down To Money
Bird On A Wire
Off To Nowhere
It Always Catches Up With You
Broken Bridges

44

A Family Man

I bet I seem a bit strange
after my radical change, to be a family man.
A lot of choices to make
and things to forsake to be a family man.
New living facilities and more responsibilities,
but I'm a family man.

My time for the things I did,
has been filled with a bunch of kids,
now I'm a family man.

Instead of driving like a fool,
I'll be shuttling kids to school,
I'm a family man.

Putting children into baths
and or working on new math,
I'm a family man.

Instead of cruising party dens

I'll be in my bed by ten (yeah, right),
I'm a family man.

Instead of sleeping in till one,
I'll have half my work day done,
I'm a family man.

It was a mutual plan, the both of us had,
a change for the good in her and me.
As for looking things through,
well I don't know about you,
but this is where I think we all aught to be.

So I won't be cruising downtown
and running all around,
I'm a family man.

Ain't trying to play it cool
while shooting midnight pool,
I'm a family man.

I don't need to strut the groove,
I got nothing there to prove,
I'm a family man.

I can't be out with you guys
till all hours of the night,
I'm a family man.

Though I'm outnumbered ten to one,
surrounded here by love,
I'm a family man.

45

It All Comes Down To Money

It all comes down to money, who you are and how you rank.
It all comes down to money and what you got in the bank.
They don't care about the cause,
working behind the scenes and above the laws.
Guns and ammo, ready to ride,
to anyone, for any war, on either side.
Puppet kings, playing their role,
while the men from miles away are in control.

And It all comes down to money, for every plane and tank.
Well, It all comes down to money and what they got in the bank.

They don't care, it's just a game.
There's lots of Keatings in this world doing the same.
Stealing from those who gave him their trust,
yet passing the deficit back on to all of us.
Taking charge, like a man of heart,
but unaccountable when it falls apart.

And it all comes down to money, how the market rose or sank.
It all comes down to money and what they got in the bank.

They don't care what we believe,
as long as they get in somehow to meet their needs.
The senator discourses his,
as the bribes and lies all speak of what he truly is.
Beyond the laws he claims to uphold,
while in somebody's pocket, already bought and sold.

It all comes down to money, who you are and how you rank.
It all comes down to money and what you got in the bank.

46

Bird On A Wire

I am a bird on a wire,
waiting for the time to expire.
Holding in my secret desire
to try,
one more time
to fly.

I'm watching the world from my perch,
I'm safe but lonely,
and lost in my search.
Still nothing can reach up
to hurt me with lies,
and disturb my flight.

I'm afraid to fly on down from here.
I want to love someone, yet I feel fear.
Every time I come down to land,
someone wants me caged
in their new plan
so I must go on,... must go on

as best I can.

Long before I fell to these ways,
I soared the skies in the joy of my days.
Never desiring to seek out a change
and be
with someone like me.

Yet change found me
on the wing far away
and I fell in love
and agreed to be caged.
I was so trusting and the victim
of rage
and war,
now I won't sing anymore.

I'm afraid
to fly on down from here.
I want to love
someone,
yet I feel fear.
Every time I come down to land,
someone wants me caged
in their new plan
and I must go on
as best I can.

I am a bird on a wire,
waiting for the time to expire.
Holding in my secret desire
to try,
one more time
to fly.

47

Off To Nowhere

We all travel the same roads, with varied highways from our home.
We all have so much in common yet we seek solitude, alone.
We all share the same purpose; the journey to love and discern.
In secret silence we meander,
instead of sharing what we've learned.
And it's off to Nowhere.
To live, to love, to find the why and where.
And it's off to Nowhere,
to find that something special out there.

Not enough time to learn it all, So much out there to see and do.
One false step and we're off the wall,
yet even this we carry through.
Not enough time to love them all, so many out there in real need.
We might reach out to heed the call,
or find another row to seed.
And it's off to Nowhere.
To live, to love, to find the why and where.
And it's off to Nowhere,
to find that something special out there.

48

It Always Catches Up
With You

Living in the shadows with your secrets on the shelf
won't help you realize you're fooling yourself.
Things have gone for years, you think you're safe, what you do,
but you don't understand, it always catches up with you.

You can run away, take leave, skip out of town,
but if you avoid the problem, it'll still hunt you down.
You can change your name, conceal what you've been through,
no matter what your precautions, it always catches up with you.

You can still pretend that everything is fine,
that the past is gone, forgotten, all covered up by time.
Just when you settle in to misconceptions of your new,
you find out the hard way, it always catches up with you.
You think that you've escaped, but you're haunted by a ghost.
You only end up hurting the ones you love the most.
So before you feed delusions that never could be true,
I hope you realize, it always catches up with you.

49

Broken Bridges

Broken bridges in high waters, Oh, I'm sinking fast.
Fallen trestle with a train coming,
and I know I just won't last.
I had my chance to speak my peace
but their ears heard not a sound.
Broken bridges in high waters and I'm leaving town.
Broken promises leave loose ends dangling,
and everybody feels in a haze.
More confused with unanswered questions
than going in separate ways.
We built a wall of peace and love, I can't see how it fell down.
Broken bridges in high waters and I'm leaving town.

The bus was too slow, the plane costs too much,
we left behind the things that we couldn't pack.
Said to my good friend Don, "I'll see you later,"
knowing I might never come back.
Dropped all commitments and got on a train
not sure just where we're bound,
Broken bridges in high waters and I'm leaving town.

50

After All These Years

So different in lifestyles, in culture and way.
Yet we grew to love each other more each day.
With nothing in common to share from the start,
save the need to find love for the lonely heart.
We were never alike, both on separate paths.
still we managed somehow to find each other at last.
After all of these years have gone by,
that fire of love still burns bright.
To live each day sharing the hopes and fears,
Together, in love, after all these years.
So much to overcome, all the differences to bare.
Yet we managed to learn to find a specialness there.
With devotion and trust, with passion to flame,
we were part of each other yet one and the same.
We were never alike, both on separate paths.
I'm sure glad in the end we found love that would last.
After all of these years have gone by,
that fire of love still burns bright.
To live each day sharing the hopes and fears,
Together, in love, after all these years.

51

⟊

MEMOIRS & NOTES - 13 - 'A FAMILY MAN'

Family Christmas Photo 1988

(1991) – The words to this poem, written in 1991, reflected my feelings as the father of 9 children who supposed he might be in control of the family's destiny. Lori and Chet were in high school, Elizabeth and Meridith were in junior high, Ben, Stephen and Spencer were in grade school, and Christopher and Allison were still at home. I was almost done with school at the college, I had a job working for the Washington State Parks Department and I just kind of felt like I was doing something right, you know, this father thing.

I thought of some of the things that helped to define or shape just what it was to make me that family man, and I came up with a few constants, like commitment and responsibility, but moreover, I thought about what many others might think as a little thing or unnecessary and tried to include a week in the life of the Baldwin family.

This poem start off with a line, **"I bet I seem a bit strange after my radical change"** which in fact, reflected one of my first struggles in fatherhood. I used to love to get stoned, smoke some pot and listen to music. And it wasn't until after Chet was born that I realized that I was a family man and that some choices were going to have to be made and some things were going have to be forsaken if I was going to do this father thing right.

Most of my childhood I had my mother's third husband, Senior as the role model of father, but he not only didn't like having to take responsibility for boys that weren't his, but he was an angry Italian alcoholic that loved his wine by the gallon. He had little to no tolerance for mistakes and a short fuse for all of his stepchildren,... And he did not interact with me on any of my interests,... like the talent shows I was in, my Boy Scouts pursuits, he never showed up for any of my football games, or any of my wrestling matches or for that matter, he never showed up for anything I was involved with,... and when I was home, with a ruthless eye for detail, he scrutinized everything I did and said, and as a teenager, I was not able to drive or even to get a driver's license. When I did something that displeased him, I was always being put on restriction, sometimes without a working timeframe, meaning I would be on restriction till it pleased him to let me off. I feared him all my childhood and was happy when we finally left him in 1967.

At the time, (1976), if I wanted to get stoned I would kind of sneak out into the garage smoke a number and then kind of slither back into the house. It was during one of those times, I was out in the garage getting ready to turn on when I thought myself, "How long can this keep going on like this? Is this what I really want my life to be like, hiding out in the garage to get stoned?" It was at that moment, that defining moment, that I made the decision to let it go. It was not an easy decision to make, even though the church dictated that smoking was against "*The Word of Wisdom*," I felt a dependency and a direct relationship between my music and my high, but I also felt that my family, that is, my wife Diane and my two children deserved to have a stronger man,... a better husband,... and a better father,... maybe not like the father in "*the Waltons*," but after being raised relatively father-less, I wanted my children to have the best father that I could be and so, that was the last time I ever got stoned.

I didn't want my children to go through their childhood, fearing or even loathing their father; I wanted them to have a caring father that they could look up to, that they could be friends with; that they could learn from; a man they would be proud to say, "That's my dad."

Side Note: "A lot of choices to make and things I have to forsake." My choice to become that father figure that I envisioned in my mind had a price and unfortunately, I lost a lot of my Portland friends that felt that I was a changed person; without me getting stoned with them, I was on the outside of the hallowed circle. Over the years, I have managed to re-bridge some of those lost friendships, but some of them are gone and will never be rekindled. Realizing yet being the quintessential family man.

I had my brother Ray in mind as part of the antagonist because at the time he was rather footloose and fancy free. He would call me up, *collect*, and ask me to drop everything, leave my wife and kids for the weekend and come down to Oregon. I must say every time I got this call I was tempted, after all, I needed that connection and reinforcement to bolster my musical self-image. And yet, from it all, I resisted.

I should say, when I wrote this song, I really didn't anticipate doing much with it, but instead, it was a nice exercise and played OK on the guitar, but to me, at the time, it wasn't anything special. But when I recorded the song, it took on a whole new life of its own, capturing the feel of a parent, and the humor of daily life, and, can I say, the heart of what I wanted to put down; and I then considered it one of my best.

It All Comes Down To Money

(1992) ~ It is said that 3 percent of the people on this earth own 90 percent of the wealth, and that throughout time the rich stay rich at the expense and misfortune of the poor. When this song was written, there was a big scandal in the news about Charles H. Keating Jr., the former Lincoln savings and loan chief executive who was known for lavish spending and big salaries during his days as a chairman of American Continental Corporation.

Mr. Keating became a symbol of the savings and loan crisis of the 1980s. In March 1987, Charles Keating Jr. needed help after finding out that the government was poised to seize the Lincoln Savings and Loan. Keating was not content to wait and hope for the best, but instead he spread a lot of money around Washington. He made arrangements to set the meeting between five senators and regulators to get the government off the Lincoln Savings and Loan's back. In September of 1990 Keating was booked into Los Angeles County jail charged with 42 counts of fraud. His bond was set at $5 million. He was later convicted in federal and state courts on charges stemming from the $3.4 billion collapse of the Irvine, California based, Lincoln Savings and Loan, which American Continental owned. This was a man who supposedly had high morals and a firm integrity that brought him to this position of authority.

One of the things that angered me the most at the time was that Keating was unrepentant and curtly chastised his own accusers as he testified that the problem wasn't him or his integrity, but the fact that regulators and Congress acted unwisely, after passing ill-considered laws and administering them incompetently which resulted in the failure of many other institutions. Keating's overconfidence and pompous arrogance during the trials struck me rather funny and although there was a lot at stake, because it was a witch hunt, I never expected Keating to be convicted but he served four and a half years in prison before those convictions were overturned in 1996.

Even still, I was left with a bad taste in my mouth and an empty feeling afterwards. So, this song came out after I realized that Keating was only one of so many thousands of callous, untrustworthy people, that control the money and the decisions to spend money all over the world.

Side Note: Charles Keating, after serving 4 ½ years in prison of a 12 ½ year sentence, was cleared of all charges involving the Lincoln Savings and Loan association. The judge ruled that his conviction was unfairly tainted because several members of the federal jury improperly discussed his earlier conviction on state fraud charges. The charges in the trial and convictions of security fraud conspiracy and racketeering, which made the name of the original judge, Lance Ito, and became a major news event and political issue, were all thrown out.

Another Side Note: Lance Ito later presided over the 1995 murder trial of O. J. Simpson, at which Simpson was acquitted.

Bird On The Wire

(1975) - Right after we moved into our own home in Olympia Washington, in September of 1975, Diane went to St. Peter's hospital where my first son, Chester III was born. Lori was about a year and a half old then and stayed over at Diane's parents during the delivery time. I came home that night to an empty, quiet, lonely house. The next day I went back and forth to the hospital and such, and during one of those trips, coming into the empty house, I sat at the piano and stared out the window of our newly acquired home.

There was a single, lonely, small yellow and gray finch sitting up on the telephone wire and it appeared to me that this bird was gazing down at me for the longest time. I felt inspired to write this song after that bird and imagined he was sitting on that wire because he was shy, maybe even reluctant due to other past experiences and then, I drew the other correlations that make this song what it is. It has always been a special gift of mine to create emotional music and this song was one of those. I recorded this once before, but I feel the version on this album, with its synthetic strings and mock orchestral embellishments, came a lot closer to what I wanted that sound to be.

Side Note: In 1957 we moved from Fairbanks Alaska where Charlie was born to Iron Mountain Michigan where Senior's brother's family and where Senior's parents lived. It was there that the *SECOND BIG HURT* happened. The four of us older boys lived and commanded the second floor of the house (John called it "Our Domain"), while Senior and my mother had a bedroom downstairs and Charlie was in a crib in their bedroom.

John was the oldest but arguably David was mostly in charge because he controlled John's decisions to a great degree. This meant that when the two of them were deciding what to do, and John would suggest they get their homework done, it was David that would calmly advise that they would do better to sit around and read comics or maybe play cards and listen to the radio. John loved his radio, and David loved to listen with John to the early Rock and roll. And John, who was well versed on every artist whose record the radio was playing, was more than willing to set his homework aside. David might suggest that it would be good to include Richie and I so as to make their card games like Hearts, or Casino, or Gin Rummy or Pinochle flow better with four players, never mind the fact that David's ulterior motives were somewhat self-serving because somehow, Richie and I never seemed to be able to win any of the card games unless we were partnered with either John or David.

Arguably, my brother David, five years older than me, was not my favorite sibling. He loved to tease and would poke his little mind games at me and Richie all the time. (Perhaps that's where I get it from). When the four of us; John, David, Richie and I were together, David would, and not in a loving way, call Richie and I *the babies*, and he would treat us dismissively and even contemptuously at times for no reasons. He liked to use me to advance things to his benefit, like having me pay to go to a movie at the Braumart Theater downtown and then have me go to the backstage exit door and let him in. I never liked doing that, but it seemed that whenever he wanted to go, I would be the one to have to go with him. On the way to the theater, I would ride on the handlebar of his bike as he peddled us to the downtown area, and, riding on the handlebar of a bike is very precarious with me sitting on the bar, my hands clenched tightly to the handlebar and there's a precariousness of your feet dangling down on either side of the revolving front tire; let me say, I hated it.

As the bike rolled along, David would have this thing about giving me advice to help me get through life. It was like he had it all figured out. There were little things like don't let the bully at school know you're afraid him, or I wouldn't trust any of the Ring brothers, (a family of boys a few doors down), to, "Try to be small when you're around Senior. Be as invisible as you can possibly be, get as far away as you can, go as fast as you can without drawing attention. And even then, David could not resist agitating me out of my supposed precarious, if not, non-existent comfort zone as he would swerve over towards the back of a variety of parked cars and say, "I can't steer,... Look out!" And just before we were about to collide with the car, he would steer clear of it. Delighting in my negative reaction, he would repeat the gesture again and again until we arrived at the theater. And there was one time when he got too close and didn't pull out in time and crashed, causing me to be thrown onto the back trunk of a 53 Chevy. Seeing me roll up on the trunk, David, smiling, asked if I was alright but not waiting for my response and needing to escape the crime scene, David had me immediately get back on the handlebar of the bike to get away fast. And although he loved to tease Richie and I whenever given the chance, so as not to paint too negative of a picture of my brother David, let me say that there was another side of David that was caring, thoughtful and protective and these traits appeared only at times when I needed them to appear.

It seemed from the time that mother got remarried to Senior, David was doomed. Senior got along well enough with John, whose easy-going, agreeable and even-tempered personality caused little to no friction or threat to Senior. In fact, Senior had John come to work with him at the Standard Gas Station that Senior was managing. But David, from the beginning, was targeted as an antagonistic menace, opposed to rules, which Senior, out of love for maintaining strict control, embraced strongly, and David seemed to be impervious to Senior's intimidations which threw up a danger-up-ahead sign to Senior, who pig-headedly decided that he was not going to let this kid get the best of him and instead, he was going to have to break this kid down or else.

So it was, Senior would watch and wait for anything David did wrong and then come down hard on him, like a ton of bricks. Sometimes the punishments were justifiable because David was a curious sort that, regardless of whatever the consequences, liked to push the envelope, but his assigned punishments were not equitable or fair when compared to any of the rest of us doing that same mistake.

And then we had a new addition to the family with the birth of my sister Mary on March 4, 1958. Mother who, after having six boys, and after always wanting to have a girl, was elated, but Senior, although accepting of the circumstances, had had hopes for another boy and I saw mother have to hide her joy whenever she and Senior were together. It was weird though, seeing mother's personality and demeanor temporarily change when Senior was home,... with mother always avoiding eye contact and only speaking after being spoken to,... but when Senior was at work, and when mother was taking care of Mary, mother became open, optimistic, cheerful and contented. I thought it was strange to have two mothers to live with; the mother when Senior was home, and the mother when Senior was gone, . And I would continue to experience this duality of mother's personality for the next nine years till mother left Senior for the last time after Christmas of 1967.

Side Note To the Side Note:

Every year around Easter, Father McCarthy from the Immaculate Conception Catholic Church would give all the altar boys a small box of fifty assorted illustrated Easter cards with offering envelopes.

One evening I was sitting three steps down from the top of the stairs, sorting the illustrated cards out by pictures when suddenly I heard loud voices yelling from the bottom of the stairs. A second later, I saw David down on his hands and feet, running on all fours, helter-skelter, up the stairs, as Senior, his face, blood red, raced behind David as he was loudly yelling something inaudible and with his belt in hand, he was whipping anything he could make contact with on David's back half. Without thinking or maybe as heightened flight instincts set in, I dove to the top of the stairs and rolled to my left. I was really scared and I wanted to close my eyes but there was no time for the peril at hand forced me to keep my eyes open to stay clear of getting stirred up in the impending danger coming my way.

At the top of the landing, David tripped on the last step and fell forward, giving Senior more opportunity to flog him, but between Senior yelling at the top of his voice the whole time and him trying to keep up with David's moving target, Senior was out of breath and totally exhausted. Yet, I was keenly aware that I was still within striking range of that belt and the wrathful look on Senior's crimson face sent waves of fear and concern through me. Senior stood and breathing hard through his nose, looked contemptuously down at David and then over at me before he turned away and stepped down the stairs and out of the second-floor domain.

For only a quick moment, as David lay there breathing hard, I was crying; crying mostly for David and his pains than from my still being scared. I looked over at him, and though David's eyes were wet, there was a defiant smile on his face as if to say, "You never got me down." And I marveled at my brother's boldness, nerve and bravery. And I realized how he really felt inside; I knew he was just as scared as I was, but it was the way he could face his fears so determined and so courageous. And for only a quick moment I saw my brother David victorious.

When David suddenly got to his feet, he looked over at me and said, "It's okay, Skipper, he's gone." David laughed and said idly, "He won't be back up here tonight." David stepped over to the stairs and started picking up the scattered cards and envelopes. I wanted to be mad at David for causing the damage to some of my choice illustrated cards, but I knew that wasn't right; David was trying to escape from the wild beast and in view of the fact that I was now seeing David in a different light, I was proud to give what I could to the hallowed cause of his safety.

David was standing on the first or second step down as I came over to stand at the top of the stairs, and from where David was standing, our heads were level with each other, like we were the same height; the same age; the same problems,... and David had a questioning look on his face as he stepped up and stopped in front of me for a moment to hand me the cards and envelopes, then he turned away with a kind of calculating look on his face and went into his room and shut the door behind him.

A couple days later, the SECOND BIG HURT happened when David didn't come home. I was worried that something had happened to him but I couldn't talk to mother about it; she was frantic and seemed to jump every time the phone would ring. The tension in the air between mother and Senior was electric with tiny glints of ediginess sparking out everywhere as mother rightly blamed Senior but could say absolutely nothing and Senior who at first showed some concern but after the first day, he didn't seem to care anymore. But the inherent friction went on for over a week until mother finally got the news that David had landed at Grandma Scarbrough's house. Mother was relieved and almost happy, knowing that David was with her mother and Senior was arguably pleased to be rid of the incorrigible boy.

Tensions subsided, things calmed down, but things upstairs were bad. John was shocked that David was gone. David who undoubtedly was John's best friend. One of John's finest attributes was his ability to find a positive perspective to his problems when they arose. John kept believing that David would suddenly come to his senses and come back home, but David never did.

Last known picture ever taken of David with his family
Left to right: Charlie, Me, Richie, David & John

Richie seemed strangely silent. I even asked him a couple of times, what he thought or felt about David being gone now, but Richie always seemed to get rather distant with me before saying, "I don't know."

Besides asking mother if she'd heard from Grandma Scarbrough about how David was doing, I didn't talk too much about him being gone. It was difficult playing cards, three-handed, everything was uneven or the cards wouldn't work out. And I missed David. I even missed the David that was obviously cheating at cards, daring me to try to discover how he cheated or how he maneuvered the cards every time to his advantage. And I missed our unstable trips to the movies and the little sage advice he'd throw at me at the weirdest of times but always welcome and always seemingly timely. After a while we just seemed to get along without David, but I still secretly maintained a sense of guilt that in my eventual complacency, it was partially my fault that David never came back.

Off To Nowhere

(1988) - Prayer is a very personal thing, and although we do it in private and in public it is a different thing from one individual to another. In another sense, except for the words of inspirational leaders like the Prophets and General Authorities that reside and guide the direction of the LDS church, prayer is our only true line of communication from ourselves to the God that we believe in.

Moreover, testimonies have been born and died by the perceived answers to prayers or lack thereof. Because it is such a personal thing, and from whatever religious or theological perspective one comes from, what it means to me and what it means to you could be totally different. Of course, as a disclaimer, I have to say that there are many who profess to be religious but are only involved for their own personal gain, be it money, power or influence, but it seemed so odd to me that as we are in an eternal process of finding our self and our purpose in this vast and seemingly un-comprehendible world, we can be so alone. We're going here and there, doing the things we do; and with so many good people, all having the same good intentions and goals, even sadder that we fight over our differences instead of relishing and celebrating those diversities. And so it is left up to us as individuals or groups to find out why we're here, who we really are, where we are going from here, and if there truly is something more. It is from that quest that I had written this song, thinly veiled as the journey to nowhere, where nowhere is where we all are right now.

It Always Catches Up With You

(1983) - Mark Twain once said that telling the truth was easier because you didn't have to remember what it what was that you said. An underlying theme of this song also included the concept that the ramification of telling lies would follow you and haunt you, and perhaps invariably hurt you.

Working at a funeral home gave me a lot of different perspectives, one of which was, that perhaps, we're all being watched and that there is an accountability and reckoning to come. This is compounded by the fact that no matter what your problem is you can't run away from it, you can't hide from it, and moreover that same problem may come back and haunt you later on.

Broken Bridges

(1971) - Originally this song was written in 1971 for piano and then converted with some modifications over to guitar, and as you can see from the date, this was one of my first songs written. It is almost trite nowadays to say that I came from a dysfunctional family, and with half of all marriages failing, I am in strong company. And although I grew up in a hostile environment without a good father image, I feel I did okay pulling myself out of the tailspin I was in. Still, although I do not know the whole underlying reasons for the breakup of my mother and father, for some time I maintained a strong resentment over the breaking up and divorce that my mother and father went through.

This song documents some of my feelings and actual events that I went through; the many times that mother left Senior as well as my own father. Unfortunately, when a divorce happens to a couple that has children, there is a whole different dimension that comes with this separation, and unfortunately, the children become the victims of the whole circumstance.

Side Note: the last lines in this poem talk about saying goodbye to my good friend Don Williams who befriended me at a time in my life when I had run out of friends. Don had brain cancer in early 1967 which left big purple scares on his head from the radiation-therapy. Because of this, Don was an oddity whose friends backed away, leaving him with a small group of people who accepted, and he could be embarrassingly obnoxious when he was around girls. There were times when I'd be with him and he would embarrass me to watch him and his cowboy moves with that overconfident poker Bob's voice.

For many years, I have wondered what ever happened to Don Williams, who lived in the Belle Acres Trailer Park in Glendora California. At this point in my life, after so many years have passed; me here with my own family. I am truly embarrassed and ashamed to say that I never found out where Don moved to and his circumstances, but to this day, I still thank him for that desperately needed friendship and love, I do wish him well.

After All These Years

(1991) - It surprises me when I think back at all the hassles, problems, mishaps and miscommunications that Diane and I experienced, but overall, we have managed to keep that wonderfulness that we have to-gether, for all these years. We were never alike, we were both on separate paths, but somehow, we managed to put the best within us both into a relationship, a marriage and family has grown more precious as time has gone on. I am truly amazed that the fire in our relationship is still powerful, but I think it has something to do with the kind of person Diane is, contrasted or complicated or complemented by the kind of person I am. A celebration and acknowledgement of that powerful fire that is still in our relationship after all these years.

52

14 - ANOTHER ONE OF THOSE DAYS - 1992

53

NOTES ABOUT THE COVERS

Okay, so I took the original album cover, reversed it, took out the, "Looks Like It's Gonna Be" from, "Looks Like It's Gonna Be Another One Of Those Days" to just be, "Another One Of Those Days," which gave me more room to make the lettering larger, did not embellish the title with a lot of gradient color, (although I did want to), made the,

"Lord Baldwin" larger and not a font I was used to, but it worked, and that's about

it.

Side Note: the, "Looks Like It's Gonna Be Another One Of Those Days" title had to go because it was just too long for publishing and took up too much space for fitting on the flip side of the album. By the way, yes, that was another Salvador Dali painting; "Apparatus and Hand" (1927) on the back cover.

170 ~ LORD CHESTER L. BALDWIN II

54

ANOTHER ONE OF THOSE DAYS

Another One Of Those Days
Why Do We Always Have To Fight?
Take The Time
This Job Is Killing Me
Reluctant For Love
I Know When It's Time To Leave
Because I Felt The Pain
Once And For All
"Another One Of Those Days,"

55

Another One Of Those Days

Dancing in the hallway, wondering out why it is,
we only got one bathroom, with this house all full of kids.
I think that I'm important but they feel the same way,
looks like it's going to be another one of those days.
No time for breakfast or lunch, so, I wave the gallant pass,
and I drive to work on an empty tank,
praying I don't run out of gas.
When I get there, nobody's got anything to say,
looks like it's going to be another one of those days.
Maybe it's a blessing, or maybe it's a curse.
I know things could be better, but they've been a whole lot worse.
I'm being optimistically here, thinking things will be fine,
but it's hard to be looking ahead
with something biting me from behind.
They say everything is attitude,
so, I'm walking around with this smile,
and I got about a hundred people
trying to take me out all the while,
but I just keep going on like I love this game we play,
looks like it's going to be another one of those days,... Yeah.

56

Why Do We Always Have To Fight?

In all of these years, we've come so far.
So much we've gone through to get where we are.
And yet we fall short and take the wrong turn.
You'd think that by now, we should have learned.
For better or worse, that's what we said.
Think out of our hearts and not our head.

So why do we waste our time tonight?
Why do we always have to fight?

This cause and effect can lead to bad scenes.
We wait for reactions to test out our means.
Both on the wrong track, we crash in the wall.
This place of depression is nowhere at all.
For better or worse, that's what we agreed.
Think out the problems and meet out the needs.

So why do we waste this time tonight?

Why do we always have to be right?
Why do we always have to fight?

In all of these years, we've come so far.
You know how we came; you see where we are.
For better or worse, learn what it's about.
You'd think that by now, we'd have this worked out.

And why do we waste our time tonight?
Why can't we just let things go by?
Why do we always have to be right?
Why do we always have to fight?

57

Take The Time

By the hands on the clock it's long time overdue.
By the signs in the street there's not much we can do.
By the writing on the wall we all share the same cause.
By the tears in your eyes you're concerned about the loss.

So why don't we do something now, are we waiting for some sign?
No one wants to end it all, so why don't we cross the line?
We all want to save the world but to take the shot is a crime.
We could do it; get involved, if we would only take the time.

By the hands reaching out, it's long time overdue.
By the homeless in the street there's so much we should do.
By the dying and the dead, it's like nobody cares; nobody cares,
and by the scenes and aftermath the proof is everywhere.

So why don't we do something now, are we waiting for some sign?
No one wants to end it all so why don't we cross the line?
We all want to save the world but we're not sure what is right.
We could do it, get involved, if we would only take the time.

58

This Job Is Killing Me

What do I owe to those in power, that never get enough?
Where will they be, what will they do
when I'm all but used up?
I work so hard to see the job get done the way I see,
yet deep inside I know the truth, this job is killing me.

This job is killing me, a little at a time.
Too much stress, too much pressure, and my life is on the line.
Can't break the chains that bind me with responsibility,
while all the while, so silently, this job is killing me.

If my performance seems to sway, they get somebody else
and I'm put out and left without to deal with life myself.
I've got to earn a living but what price to pay to eat.
A nervous breakdown and my health, this job is killing me.

This job is killing me, a little at a time.
Too much stress, too much pressure, and my life is on the line.
Can't break the chains that bind me with responsibility,
while all the while, so silently, this job is killing me.

A woman lives a much longer life for reasons still in doubt.
But I might speculate the facts are not hard to figure out.
Am I the stupid fool or what to allow this all to be?
I feel the weight, I know the signs, this job is killing me.

This job is killing me, a little at a time.
Too much stress, too much pressure and my life is on the line.
Can't break the chains that bind me with responsibility,
while all the while, so silently, this job is killing me.

59

Reluctant For Love

Struggling so hard to find who I am.
Answers are riddles,
my faith is a sham;
my confidence sways.

I can't understand what all of this means,
I'm always confused,
my future just seems
so distant and vague.

I don't want to live my life in loneliness
Isolated and left all alone.
I don't want to live my life in loneliness,
but I'm so afraid,
I just stay home.

Lost and unsure when a chance finally nears.
My heart full of hope,
but clouded by fears,
I'm reluctant for love.

I don't understand what makes me so shy,
afraid to be bold, afraid to just try
to reach out for love.

I'd like the same chance for happiness to shine on me.
I can't continue like this,
but I don't know how to break free.

I don't want to live my life in loneliness
isolated and left all alone.
I don't want to live my life in loneliness,
but I'm so afraid,
I just stay home.

All of my life I thought there would be
some special person out there for me a
nd knows what to do.

Ready for love, should it pass by my way
hoping I'll find
the courage to say
I need you too.

60

I Know When It's Time
To Leave

It's such a big joke, the way you changed your mind.
All those words you spoke were related to a different time.
But don't turn away like you're so naïve,
because I know when it's time to stay
and I know when it's time to leave.

You've gone out of your way to avoid facing me.
Is it so hard to relate to changes from what used to be?
I can't really say what I truly believe
but I know when it's time to stay,
and I know when it's time to leave.

I know about your friend and the plans you've gone through.
If this is really the end, I wish you could have told me too.
but you won't have to play that ace up your sleeve,
I know when it's time to stay,
and I know when it's time to leave.

Take no promise to heart and how could you miss?
Still I wish we'd part on a different note than this.
But I'll be on my way by early eve
Babe, I know when it's time to stay,
and I know when it's time to leave.

61

Because I Felt The Pain

So I stayed up real late at night, to write these songs for you.
Though you were nowhere close in sight, I felt you might approve.
I wrote them for you with care, though I never chanced to share
concern with you, and yet, what's fair is fair.

And with a tear I sang my song, for the joys and for the griefs.
I hoped that you might sing along to be part of my beliefs.
For someone said it should, as one who feels the grain of wood.
To be recognized as good as only a sensitive one could.

And with the years passed all my time,
nothing ventured nothing gained.
With all the happenings in my life, I changed, yet still, remained
a poet with no audience to please, as winds blow the falling leaves
my friends grew older too and raised up their families.

So I stayed up real late at night, because I felt the pain.
Though you were nowhere close in sight, I felt you might sustain.
I wrote them for you with care though I never chanced to share
as we pass from here to there what's fair is fair.

62

Once And For All

It's come back to me, as I knew it would,
though I put it off for as long as I could.
There's no hiding the truth, it has to be faced,
everything in it's time, everything in it's place.
Though I swept it away, underneath the bed,
the problem is mine, and weighs on my head.
I have procrastinated to avoid this somehow,
but come to me problem, come to me now.

Once and for all, I'll see this thing through
and not have the weight of this hanging me too.
There comes a time when I stand or fall,
so I'll handle it right, once and for all.

It's come back to me, and I will be free,
when I stand strong and face things in front of me.
There's no hiding away, it's still there in my sight,
everything in its place, everything in it's time.
Though I swept it away, it was still always there,
the problem is one that only I can repair.

I have procrastinated to avoid this so long,
but come to me problem, let me right the wrong.

Once and for all, I'll see this thing through
and not have the weight of this hanging me too.
There comes a time when I stand or fall,
so I'll handle it right, once and for all.

MEMOIRS & NOTES - 14 - 'ANOTHER ONE OF THOSE DAYS'

Another One Of Those Days

(1992) - Yes, I raised 10 children in a house with 1000 square feet of space and only one bathroom. The reason some of the words to this poem, (these lyrics), seems a bit disjointed is because the idea for the words to this poem came to me years earlier while I was working at JW Electronics, but I was rather stifled in my creativity (and my psyche) altogether there, and although there were notes and ideas put down, I never seemed to put it all together into one solid thing. When this poem was finally written, in 1992, Lori was a senior and Chet was a sophomore at Tumwater High School, Elizabeth and Meredith were both in Tumwater Junior High, Ben, Stephen and Spencer were all in Black Lake Elementary and Allison was a baby still at home. Life ain't always easy, even when we work at it real hard at making it that way.

There were many early mornings as we'd need to go to seminary, where Chet and I were totally locked out of the bathroom, and the use of any of its facilities as Lori got ready for Seminary (where we and two other families took turns driving to the church) and Liz and Meridith would be in the bathroom getting ready to catch the bus to go to school. Back then, we still had a lot of trees behind us, so Chet and I would find ourselves watering the bushes before he would be picked up to go to Seminary and I then had to go to work. Sometimes it was almost like a routine where I would get up, go outside and take a leak, come back in, get ready and go to work, and never see any of the girls. Oh, I could hear them in there with the water running, the toilet flushing, the hair dryers blowing, sometimes them arguing, some-times laughing, sometimes singing along with one of Lori or Liz's "mix" cassettes in the player, but I never saw them, and if I did, I was usually never given access to the use of the facilities.

The words to the poem also reflects the post-work syndrome that I was going through while working at JW Electronics, where I was making some money but I had little to nothing to spend and I would find myself driving to work looking down at the gas gauge which indicated I was running on empty, knowing I had no money and I still had to get back home. Moreover, when I did get to work, because everyone was so worried about the possible closing of the store, there was a lot of speculation, secretive and covert operations going on, and I had little to no conversation with anyone. And then there was my motivation, which vacillated on how I was feeling that particular day, self-worth wise, where I felt if I was optimistic, others might follow, but in the end, some of my coworkers that were clearly stations above me, meaning I could be no threat, even they could be dismissive, and a few that did not like me could be dubiously mistrusting, thinking there was some other thing going on, and they would became defensive, even downright offensively unpleasant to me at times,...

"They say everything is attitude, so I'm walking around with this smile,
and I got about a hundred people trying to take me out all the while,
but I just keep going on like I love this game we play,
looks like it's going to be another one of those days."

..., and there were many times as I was up against the wall or turning my head ever so slightly to use my peripheral vision to see the true way someone felt about me or something I did or said, that I would find myself thinking, "Looks Like It's Going To Be Another One Of Those Days."

Side Note:

I really loved the harmonica in this piece,... it just made the whole song cook that much hotter. The neat thing is, it was so comfortable or natural and laid-back to syncopate with the melody. It makes me tap my feet to it without even listening to the composition.

Why Do We Always Have To Fight?

(1992) - This would seem to be a simple question that a couple might ask themselves, especially if they can get past their presupposed notions and their self-imposed prejudices and pride; baggage that, unfortunately, we all carry with us. I am no different than any other man who wishes to be listened to when I feel there is a problem, and Diane is no different than any other woman who wishes to be really heard and understood when there is a problem.

By the time this poem was written, I was already back to work at SPSCC, and money was coming in, but I was an 11-month employee which meant that when the college was closed, in between the end of summer quarter and the beginning of fall quarter, I was out of work and we had no money coming in for that time period.

It may be true that most arguments between married couples have something to do with money, or lack of money, and that was rightly our problem at times, but I also believe that it all comes down to communication skills. We went through some harried times not just during that month off, but because school is starting, property taxes were due and a lot of hidden expenses seem to come out and around at that time.

Make no mistake, we were hurting, and although Diane did her best to work with what money was coming in, there were times that her frustration and unhappiness with our financial circumstances came to a head. That unhappiness, along with our breakdown of communications would sometimes find us resorting to anger as seemingly the only alternative.

The words to this poem implies that after a time couples should have learned from their mistakes and be able to recognize from the signs that there's a problem and maybe even fix the problem, but sometimes, due to financial circumstances or circumstances beyond our control, if the situation continues even though it may be no one's fault, the problem is nonetheless still a challenge that needs to be dealt with, sometimes over and over again, but understanding that this problem is something we need to try to get control over is an important step, and I would consciously find myself asking the question, "why do we always have to fight?"

Take The Time

(1991) - The lyrics mirror a frustration with the lack of concern for the breakdown of the ecological and environmental circumstances of the world. Working for the Parks department, I was surrounded by ecological and environmental extremists that hoped to bring the world to some awareness of the problems of our country and our world. For all the good intentions, sometimes their statements followed by their apathy, would send a conflicting message to me and anyone associated with them.

Still, sympathy for a needed, but less recognized cause, as well as empathy with another's misfortunes is one thing, affecting a plan for some type of plausible solution and or change is altogether another thing. And so, the words of this poem reflect that person's frustration with a set of circumstances from the impending signs they see or are dealing with, along with their confusion and unhappiness over just what to do while trying to make something happen to affect the needed change for the better.

This Job Is Killing Me

(1991) – In my past I have perhaps, had unwarranted devotions to some of the places I worked for, in spite of the fact that most of the places I worked for returned little to no loyalty, dedication or commitment to me. At JW Electronics (15 plus years), I was paid poorly, had little benefits, was treated poorly partially because I did not drink or smoke, which excluded me from the boy's club that met every night after work to talk shop and drink by cases, Rainier beer (which came in bottles, so the next day I would go dumpster diving to pull them out and get the deposits on them), and partially because I was a scrounge. So, drawing from the, now, maybe-to-some famous words of the Concorde Hotel kitchen Bimmy who was pulling out a rack of newly cleaned scalding hot plates from the industrial Hobart dishwashing machine, and replying curtly to my feeble complaint about the terrible staff food, which was comprised of all the leftover food that could not yet again be disguised and recycled into another meal for the guests, he stopped stacking the plates for a second and said, "You don't like it; you quit."

One night while watching one of the evening news programs there was a segment about working people in Japan. This 10-minute segment talked about the working conditions of the people in Japan along with the social, psychological, spiritual and temporal ramifications of those conditions.

Due to an overwhelming need of a person in Japan to keep their job, most of these workers would stay on the job, sometimes overnight, or work for days on end without making contact with their own families. Perhaps the most concerning information about this news article was the fact that many of these people valued their jobs above their families and even their own personal health. People were literally working themselves to death.

Side Note:

Even before I got out of high school, I was making conscientious life choices early on towards my varied opportunities of employment, like choosing between Burger Chef Management or being a Laborer for a construction company in Portland that built highway bridges. The money was twice as much but the danger level to damaging my fingers to possibly take me out of my ambition to be a songwriter musician that needed those hands for playing guitar and piano outweighed the money. Then there was the Georgia Pacific job where, at first, I thought this will be great. It's a no-brainer job, I can do my eight hours of work and think of lyrics to new songs, but working next to and with powerful metal machines that I was careful not to get too close to. And there was a lot of other moving parts to the warehouse like the unforgiving fork-lift drivers driving way too fast in front of me, by me, and behind me, all the time, even though I was on my side of the safety line, I almost got run over, twice. And so it went, I continued to find work where my body was not too punished for the sake of paying the bills. Honestly, I was always thinking somebody would discover the wonderful music and lyrical poetry material I was cranking out and that I would be justified in my previous, less-than-lucrative career choices. Forty years later and I'm still working at getting noticed.

Reluctant For Love

(1988) – After I left high school, and all through my lonely single life I thought that somewhere out there in that big world there was a special person looking and maybe dreaming of someone to come along in their life, maybe like me. And, like me, maybe that person would be ready for the commitment and responsibility of love and companion-ship. And I felt, should the opportunity pass by my way, I would not only recognize that opportunity, but I would conquer my shyness, she might overcome hers, and together we would find a special commonality that we could build a lifetime relationship with.

It was on a cold January or February night; I was riding back from the Ongford Apartments where Diane lived

to my own apartment a couple miles away.

As I pedaled, I said a prayer in which I commented to Heavenly Father that I thought maybe Diane was the one, and as I was just kind of praying, I was overcome by the Spirit that, regardless of how I felt unworthy, washed over the center of my being, and confirmed to me, that she was the one.

Side Note:

Diane once confided in me that if I had not come along, she might not have gotten married and might even have spent her life living alone. Because I know her heart, I took that feeling—that possible quiet desperation and wrote these lyrics. I never told her about the correlation, nor do I think that she has ever made any association, but I feel that the kind, goodness and sensitiveness of the character in the song shines through.

I Know When It's Time To Leave

(1991) – There are some clichés that just seem to beg me to put music to poetry to create a song. When I first played this song to Diane, her enthusiasm to the tune and lyrics motivated me to make this one of my performing pieces. And in public, this was well received. But this was one of those songs that was recorded, re-recorded and then re-recorded again, but because of the odd timing and syncopation, I could never truly capture the ambience or spirit of this piece. I think if I recorded this in a studio with other musicians the brightness of the energy of this song might improve the piece and shine through.

Side Note:

My mother had made a really poor choice in divorcing my dad to marry this other guy (Senior), that would get oftimes get drunk on wine and then lose control of his civility and good manners and get physical with her and or her children. For me, it was time to leave when we were too scared to go down to the first floor of the house knowing we would have to confront Senior. It was time to leave when Senior would lose control and strike out at anyone in his way. It was time to leave when I saw mother would have to put on extra makeup on her face to cover the bruises inflicted by Senior after he lost control. Two years into her marriage with Senior and after the first year in Iron Mountain Michigan, after we all got to know Senior from his wide, mood-swinging behaviors, his disproportionate and sometimes crewel discipline, unpredictable methods of getting the punishments served for whatever crime was or was not committed, it was always time to leave.

Because I Felt The Pain

(1977) – The poet in me wants to think that it is the most important part of this partnership called songwriting, and the musician in me begs to differ with it, saying that it is in fact the music that is the most important factor in the creation of songs. Doesn't matter, sometimes one faction has it over the other and sometimes they gel together so well that I look and wonder how it all happened.

Before I got the keyboard where the sound can be concealed with the use of a headphone, I had the piano, or to be precise, my mother's piano. This piano had lived for fifty years with Grandma Scarbrough, until she passed away in 1973, and then it fell to me, with the thought that if my mother ever wanted it, she would have it. Fast forward three years later, the piano was now out in my living room in Olympia Washington.

Of course, the only time I had to really compose songs was after everyone went to bed where I could create compositions without bothering anyone. And so it was for years, if I was impressed to create, it would have to be at the expense of my sleep. I didn't mind it too much though; it was the price I'd have to pay and because I was young, it wasn't so bad.

Without knowing how to write music down, songs can be a fleeting thing, here tonight, gone tomorrow morning thing. This was a time when I was without a tape recorder and so, after I would write the poem, I would sit at the piano and hope that something came to me, and when it did, I would have to stay up and play the piece over and over until I had the composition memorized in my fingers and in my head.

There was no shortcut to this process, and yet, I was not daunted by this apparent inconvenience, I just did what came to me, and I was usually thankful to Heavenly Father for the inspiration.

It was a Monday night, February 13th 1977, Lori was three and Chet was 14 months old. It was late because we had a problem getting those two kids to go to sleep. So it was already late in the evening when I was sitting at the piano, trying desperately to write a love song for Diane for Valentine's Day.

And although I was trying, jotting down notes and stanzas, nothing of substance was coming out. Then I heard the sound of a baby crying and went to Chet's crib and delivered Chet to his mother so he could nurse. Diane woke up just enough to adjust putting the baby in our bed before she went back to sleep.

I went back to the piano, pounded out a few chords, but I wasn't feeling anything but sleepy. I made a soft noise from the piano as I softly laid my arms over the piano keys and laid my head on top of my hands to rest for just a moment. But I fell asleep. I woke up about two or three in the morning with drool running out of my mouth and little dents from some of the black keys impressed into my face.

I thought then of the price that I had to pay sometimes, just to write these songs that nobody besides my immediate family would ever listen to. For whatever reason, it suddenly occurred to me that this subject itself could possibly be the beginning of a song. Now I had a purpose; this song was for Diane; I would write a poem about what I was thinking, feeling about while writing this song. Thus, the words in the first verse of the poem reflect that one desire to write the song even though there is a price to pay. The second verse speaks of my passion and desire to add the emotion and feeling to those words and music, and for the purpose;

"I wrote them for you **(Diane)**, *with care,"*

which would be alright even if the rest of the world was totally oblivious to it; this song was for Diane. The words to the third stanza of the poem looks at the songwriter himself (or herself), the musician and the poet as they collaborate and think about and muse, as to what it is they are doing and why. In the fourth stanza, the words to the poem reflects on and tries to reinforce that answer, as well as coming to the realization that, the appreciated or unappreciated or celebrated or un-recognized songs that are written by me, are ultimately also written for me or for myself as well, and in doing so, it kind of justifies my actions in some small way and perhaps recognizes the small sacrifices, and or the reasons, for me to be pursuing this peculiar path of life.

Side Note:

It took me two more hours to complete the lyrics and to memorize the fingering for the piano music. As the emotion and timbre of the song got to me, the piece started to flow, and though there were tears in my eyes because the song was so moving to me, I was not holding back, meaning, I would ignore my discomfort and awkwardness to let this song flow from my heart.

When I began yet again, I was playing the piano quietly, (pianissimo) then without knowing, I graduated to average, (mezzo-piano forte) but towards the end of my practice, I was there playing (forte). I was sure that by then, Diane would have come out to the living room to see why I was so loud and then, get her special Valentine Day present. But she did not. When I finished a final run through, I looked at the clock and seeing it was after three, debated whether or not I should go back to sleep because I had to go to work that morning.

When I came home that evening, Diane had made me a special

dinner of lasagna and French bread, and a Cherry pie. After dinner we put the two kids to bed and I was preparing to play the new song for Diane, when the baby woke back up. Diane went to nurse Chet in the rocking chair in the living room but, you guessed it, Diane went to sleep. After a long period of their sleeping time, I put Chet back in his crib and went out to the living room but Diane was not there. I found that she left to put on her nightclothes and was lying in bed. I talked softly to her, encouraging her to come out into the living room, but when she answered in gibberish, I knew the evening was done. I went into the kitchen and cut myself a big piece of that cherry pie and sat on the couch, watching an episode of Star Trek, (the original series).

Now, the next night, after dinner while she was rocking Chet to sleep, I told her about the new Valentine Day song that I had written for her, and said, "I'd like to play it for you before you go to sleep." I then promptly played the song for her. When I finished playing, I looked over at her and saw that she looked kind of embarrassed and had tears in her eyes. I thought to myself, "Mission accomplished."

Once And For All

(1984) – Although there were many wonderful things that happened to me after I started working at Forest Funeral Home, I did have a few problems that I never shared with anyone. This poem, in its elusive lyrics, reflects one of those problems. My intention was to go to work at the funeral home until something else came along. You know, that is kind of like life, in that there are a lot of plans that you may have and ideas that you want to bring to pass, but along the way, life happens and then, how you deal with that thing called, "life," as it happens, makes all the difference to your character and your psyche.

I did get the hang of this thing, being a funeral director, and I could talk with families that were in stressful circumstances, and with sincerity and concern, I was great.

Doing the necessary services for the family, and by that, I mean doing everything; like doing the involved city and state government paperwork, making the arrangements, (funeral\cremation\burial, other?), doing the notices and the obituary, and even officiating sometimes at the funeral home services in our chapel, or officiating at a memorial service at a church. Anyway, I figured this whole thing out, and I was doing what I felt, was a really good job.

But deep inside unbeknownst to anyone, I had this fear, every time I did an embalming. It wasn't because I had to cut into their dead skin, although at first, I had to have some, "getting used to it" time. And my fears did not stem from having a hard time digging with my fingers into the fascia and muscle tissue to get to the veins to pull out the arteries, no, my fears, which stemmed from my first three encounters with cadavers, was when that individual's remains would not embalm properly. Embalming chemicals have a variety of preservatives, sanitizers, disinfectant agents, and additives is known as embalming fluid, used to temporarily delay decomposition and hopefully restore a natural appearance for the viewing of a body after death.

The first body that I ever embalmed by myself, that is to say without someone looking over my shoulder, was this 97-year-old woman that had died in a Bremerton hospital and then put into a refrigeration unit for storage until I went up there to pick up her remains. After I got her all set up on the table and broke the rigor that had set in, I made the incision, dug down and searched "in vain," (sorry, kind of a joke), for the carotid artery located on the right side of the neck, and finally, after many minutes of digging around, I finally pulled out the artery, only to find that it lacked the elasticity needed for my operation. Still, I struggled with that entry point and finally got some push results, but the results were hot so visibly apparent, especially in the limbs.

Next, I tried a right subclavian artery which did not seem to do anything, (and I was worried that I wasn't really in the right vein), Then I did an axillary by doing an incision inside the arm pit, on the right arm going both directions. This did work except for her hand which was blotchy and discolored. So, then I had to do a radial, (artery in the wrist) to get the color results I that needed. There were many other incisions I had to make and I was there until 4 in the morning making sure this one came out right.

Unfortunately, the next week that followed, I had two more bodies that were really close in age and condition to that 97-year-old woman. The first was an old man that had been dead for two days before he was discovered, and the other was a woman who had arterial sclerotic disease, which of course made embalming a nightmare because there was no circulatory system.

Side Note:

After a one-time perfect embalming, I had three in a row that caused me high anxiety, two of them were so bad from sclerotic lesions in the coronary arteries and their epicardial branches that I had to do multiple attempts from different entries to get past their clogged-up Circle of Willis, have to put embalming-fluid-soaked cotton packs on their faces and hands to get the preferred outcome. They all turned out great and the families were pleased with the results, but this embalming thing was not something I wanted to continue doing.

Another Side Note:

The long and short of this whole story is that I had to work real hard every time I embalmed any cadaver's corpse and I always had this fear; this deep-down unsettling fear, that something was going to go wrong and that I was not going to be able to embalm this body, and even worse, that person's remains would look terrible after the embalming, which of course would not only be a travesty to the family who paid good money for me to be doing the job, but would also reflect on my inability to do the job that was hired for. I wrote the lyrics to this poem because I needed to overcome this fear and finally standup once and for all.

64

17 - VOICES -1993

65

NOTES ABOUT THE COVERS

I was recording almost every day when I recorded this album, "Voices From The Past," and I was having fun. In a numbered sequence, we skipped from album 14, to Album 17 because album 15, "No Words Tonight," (not published yet) and 16, "Somewhere In My Life," are both experimental albums, and strictly instrumentals.

Around October of 1992, George Michael, British singer-songwriter had filed suit to sue his record la-bel Sony Music Entertainment. At the time; George Michael was claiming he did not have the freedom to do what he wanted with his eight-album con-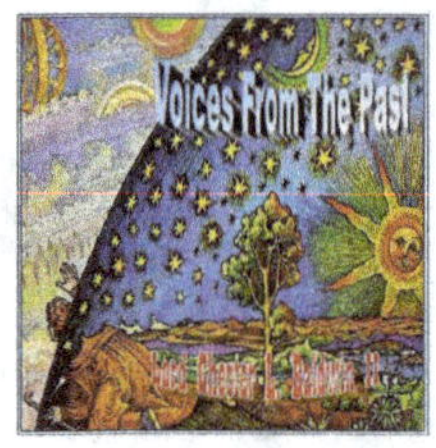tract, that SONY prevented him from managing his professional image, and that he had little control over his work; remarking that SONY was treating him as, "no more than a piece of software."

This was really all about money, and I wish George Michael all the best, but his situation did make me think about how cool it was that I had complete freedom to do whatever I wanted with my material.

As I got more involved with my Yamaha PSR-500 keyboard, and

improved my guitar work, I started adding extra spontaneous stuff to some of my songs with quirky but stimulating beginnings and then extensive endings. This gave me the chance to experiment past the melodies and the trailing off exits with whatever lead instrument I would play with, and my harmonica solos could go longer than eight bars, allowing me to extend the beginnings and endings when I so wished; giving me more freedom to experiment with off-beat sounds, altering and transforming the whole package, And so I did, and I did it because I could

Over there is a look at what the album looked like in 1992. This is, of course, a coloured copy of, "The Flammarion Engraving," The artist is unknown, but I didn't want to take any chances of slowing my progress down by finding this was somehow copyrighted, you all know about, 'Getty Images,' right?.

66

VOICES FROM THE PAST

Voices From The Past
I Love This Job
Just Passing Through
Something For The Pain
The Day After Tomorrow
Carried Away
Blow Up The TV

67

Voices From The Past

They came before with hopes and dreams;
desires for the chance to be.
Faint traces of a person, cast from sketchy letters and photographs.
And yet, I feel I know their same, for reasons I can not explain.
And of these folks, who they might be
and of their passions and of their dreams.
I feel they hoped their cause would last,
to speak as voices from the past.
As I delve further, that I may see, the voices softly call to me
and beckon me to find their role, their motivations of the soul.
And how could I ignore my kin, all they were or might have been?
And of these folks, who they might be, are still part of my family.
They call to me, with subtle cast and speak as voices from the past.
I see a face and relate a name, passed down stories that remain.
I touch a part still close at hand
and I want to know who was that man?
But now I run, it is my day, to carry heritage on its way.
And of these folks, I know and see, all wait beyond the Veil for me.
Their ties and bonds, forever last to speak as voices from the past.

68

I Love This Job

Here I am, major leagues after a long, hard go.
It wasn't easy to change but I had support at home.
Now, I'm working at a job and doing what I want.
don't make a lot of money, but I have a lot of fun.

I love this job and how I spend my time,
I go to work happy, come home feeling fine.
I don't have to lie, back-stab, cheat or rob,
just do my best, I love this job.

We all made sacrifices for this dream to come true.
There was lots of doing without for a time or two.
College and working two jobs, day and night.
so we could land the big one and do what we like.

I love this job and how I spend my time,
I go to work happy, come home feeling fine.
I don't have to lie, back-stab, cheat or rob,
just do my best, I love this job.

Seems like a big hassle and I won't say it's not,
but if you work just to exist, then what have you got?
You live with yourself and you have to be up-front,
why not put all your energy into doing what you want?

You can love your job and how you spend your time,
go to work happy, come home feeling fine.
You don't have to lie, back-stab, cheat or rob,
just do your best, and love your job.

69

Just Passing Through

Watching it all go by. Lost are the reasons why.
Reasons of what for, don't matter anymore.
Only one thing seems to me, a strong sense of urgency.
Are my footprints big in size for any to recognize?
My big moment of being new, just passing through.
The time lines that go on there, circle back and touch somewhere.
Yet, we're locked within a track, and we never can turn back.
All the vague realities, lost within some history
are documentations of truth, stained by someone's point of view.
still, I'm looking for the true, just passing through.
And me, in my search to find, what do I leave behind,
for all that search of me, for my posterity?
Words for songs left unsung, beginnings of the deeds undone.
As my children ask in doubt, "what was he all about?"
There's so much to be and do, while just passing through.
Call to task and try to determine what to stand by.
Leaving a trail to see, for those that follow me.
Hoping some prints might remain, after tides have washed away,
down the shores of what was me, in the halls of eternity.
Otherwise, I'm just like you, just passing through.

70

Something For The Pain

Headlines, bread lines, the homeless in the streets.
Hardships, conflicts, cops walking the beat.
Fat rats, cool cats, playing hard in the sham.
Bad boys, sad ploys, with victims of the scam.

Cold leach, dead beat, danger, out of bounds.
Cultures, vultures, make the daily rounds.
Destitute, weak youth drawn into the lure,
find something for the pain, nothing for the cure.

Banquets, benefits, the charities that care.
Close call, green wall, all that you can spare.
Sinister, ministers, prey while you pay.
Good cause, outlaws, too many pockets on the way.

Hard times, dark signs, the child with a gun.
Bare feet, blood street, kids on the run.
Promises, ominous, with authorities unsure,
that's something for the pain, nothing for the cure.

Big bust, silent rust, bad boys going down.
Lawyer make, judges take, control of the town.
Cat walk, deadlock, guilty running free.
Innocent, money spent, for what, nobody sees.

Fool's play, big pay, but for who or what?
Charmed life, sharp knife, ready for the cut.
Short walk, long talk, just the main-street tour,
it's something for the pain, nothing for the cure.

71

The Day After Tomorrow

And it seems that things could be a lot better,
but they've been worse at times so I've no room to complain.
All our dreams are put off for sometime later,
always slipping back, it's hard to see any gain.

But one of these days we'll break free from these conditions.
Lay down these long days of the farm,
the tractor and harrow.
God willing, and the creek don't rise
and before this good hope dies,
we might see it all come true
the day after tomorrow.

Just because we're in the trap of the debtor,
owing more than we can make, working twice as hard to stay on.
The way it was, farming life was much better,
not giving into speculation till everything's gone.

But one of these days we'll be free to grow what we want to,
not practice poverty in between the banking and borrow.

God willing, and the creek don't rise
and before this good hope dies,
we might see it come to pass
the day after tomorrow.

They say that farming life is easy, but that's a myth.
Bills need attention with nothing to pay them with.
Had to plow some crop turned bad, back in the ground.
The tractor, acting funny, is making a new sound.
With the well run dry, had to truck water to the field.
With the spring so poor, looks like we won't get much yield.
The bank wants to step in but we ain't leaving without a fight.
Only get ten percent for the land to the fly by night.

Seems we fall into hard times without even knowing,
between a rock and a hard place, with everything going wrong.
Through it all, we've managed to keep things going,
I guess the opposition has helped to build us up strong.
But one of these days we'll break free from these conditions.

Lay down these long days of the farm, the tractor and harrow.
God willing, and the creek don't rise
and before this good hope dies,
we might see it all come true
the day after tomorrow.

72

Carried Away

Sad times, troubled child, where are all of their good friends?
Hopeless dreams, desperate moves, means to justify ends.
Long trials, quick decisions, read out between the line.
Parents turn from their position, and say they don't have time.
What about love and concern for the child brought to earth?
What do we teach, what do they learn,
if not their own special worth?
Sent to schools, taken to church but at home stored on the shelves.
How can we love and know a child if we're hung up on our selves?
Lost in the day, carried away.
Sad thoughts, troubled teen, just one step behind the rest.
Hopeless future, desperate means, just to stay up with the rest.
No guidance, no support, running scared, confused alone.
Mom and Dad working full time, just to keep hold of their home.
What about quality time for the child brought to earth?
If we don't teach, then they don't learn of their own special worth.
Send them to schools, take them to church,
but at home, starve them for love.
How can we ever know the child if we're always so hung up?
Lost and afraid, carried away.

73

Blow Up The TV

Sitting on the couch, all the evening in a haze,
staring at the screen while my mind is in a daze.
I wonder what I did last week or last year,
and I realize in fact I spent most the time right here.

The kids spend more time here than with their family line,
addicted to Nintendo long after their bedtime.
Watching reruns and old movies seen too many times before
and crash the night with pillows and blankets on the floor.

Blow up the TV, smash it from the shelves,
it's trashing our kid's minds as well as ourselves.
Blow up the TV and we will all be free.
We can get back to basics and the way we used to be.

When the cartoons in the morning are at least second rate,
hard to realize there's other people to relate.
The sun is outside shinning, so much to do yet,
but they'd rather sit and stare at the program on the set.

Soaps on in the afternoon, then hours of the news,
programs to fill up the time with so much there to choose.
One wonders in a way, what do they get from day to day,
with violence, and sex, and the role models they portray.

Let's blow up the TV, smash it from the shelves,
it's trashing our kid's minds as well as ourselves.
Blow up the TV and we will all be free.
We can get back to basics and the way we used to be.

When I don't know my kids from the comedy last night,
if all I do is argue or in fact get in a fight,
if the kids don't know each other because the TV is always on,
it time I'd say to end it all, and cry after it's gone.

Kids think life is boring for they need the exercise,
and get away from fantasies and situation lies.
Their lives all lack experience and lessons of the heart.
How will they do in life if they never do take part?

So, blow up the TV, smash it from the shelves,
it's trashing our kid's minds as well as ourselves.
Blow up the TV and we will all be free.
We can get back to basics and the way we used to be.

74

MEMOIRS & NOTES - 17 -
'VOICES FROM THE PAST'

Voices From The Past

(1990) – Our genealogical work is closely related to our recognizing the ties from our past and our ties to

the future. I think most people are genuinely interested in their genealogy. The first thought that came to me, was that within all these old photographs and pictures, all those faces that were, for what ever reason, frozen

in time onto those glossy pieces of paper, from those historical slices of time, there is an individual, a person that had had passions, desires, fears, joys, loves,

Grandma and Grandpa
Scarbrough

and, I don't know, dreams of their own. It just kind struck me, that at one time while they were here on this earth, in many ways they were just like me. And I didn't know them; not really, I mean, even my own grandparents; Grandma and Grandpa Scarbrough, I didn't really know who these people were, and I was too busy being a kid to even try to understand what was going on in their lives, what it was that they wanted out of life and what they hoped to accomplish in their lives. And I envisioned, as I looked at the pictures, I imagined those people looking back at me, almost calling out and saying, hey there, come find me; come find out about what I was all about. Lately, another thought that has been haunting me

Grandma & Grandpa Snook

is that, someday, someone will be looking at pictures of me and wonder who was this guy, and what was it that he wanted out of life? On that second question, it was my hope to expound a little bit more on that idea. And after all, ain't we all just temporarily doing that whatever thing it is that we do here on this earth; ain't we all, *"Just Passing Through?"*

I Love This Job

(1991) - After spending 13 years working at JW Electronics in its rough, unapologetic, dog-eat-dog environment, (of which I was guilty of tolerating for too long), you'd think I would have figured out what my problem was, but I endured the hardship, not just for the money and the promise of that better tomorrow, (which never happened), but I was guilty of not only feeling that I was not good enough to do something else, but I continued following the path of least resistance, and guilty of not speaking up when I was being oppressed, demoralized, exploited, and downtrodden. But mostly, it was my fault for not preparing myself when I was younger for my own future, as well as my family's.

When I got the job and went to work at the Washington State Parks Department it was a real game changer. All of a sudden, I was working on projects, and from newly learned skills that I had acquired from college classes, I was working with and on my own terms, and I now had people I was responsible for, people needing and asking for my advice, (which rarely happened at JW), and now I was able to use some new tools; knowledge of computers, network systems, I used some life skills that I had accumulated and honed while at Forest Funeral home, and with the confidence that, within this new change in environment, I was on a swifter learning curve than ever before, where I wanted the diverse challenges so I could overcome them and learn in the process. Suddenly, I really liked going to work, in fact I even liked staying there after work, even if I wasn't getting paid. Like Gary Rook at Forest Funeral Home, I was treated with great respect, and my opinion and my work was valued, and moreover I was not only appreciated for the kind of work that I was doing, but I was appreciated for the person I was. All of this was a stark difference from my days at JW Electronics. Suddenly with me in a career track, learning new things, making new friends, making better money than ever before, life was good.

Just Passing Through

(1988) - During the hippie movement in the '60s Robert Crumb, who was an underground comic book artist, had this character he created named, Mr. Natural. Mr. Natural was kind of a parody of the Maharishi Mahesh Yogi who was an Indian guru, known for developing the Transcendental Meditation technique and for being the leader and guru of a worldwide organization that the Beatles and Donovan went to visit for enlightenment. One of the characterizations of Mr. Natural was the picture of him stepping towards you in that "trucking" kind of gate with him waving to you and saying "just passing through." For years I have carried on and used that same catch-all phrase, "just passing through" to epitomize how a person might feel when that, he or she might project their all-too-serious perspective of their religion, life, love, and I feel at times, the desire for us all to just lighten up. And when conversations drift to fear of failure, of existentialism gone array, or fatalism and why we exist on this certain plane at this time, or dwelling on the concept of how fleeting our mortal life can seem, lackadaisically I could say, "Hey there, brother, we're all just passing through."

Following the theme of the album itself, I wrote the lyrics to this song with some of the same perspectives and questions of life, of why we're here, and I envisioned myself on that endless circle of time, coming back around to where I've already been, and trying to put together some perspective of my place in my time, but also my place in the generations of my relatives. This heritage, through our genealogy is where we as individuals try to fit in by associating ourselves with our immediate family and our kin or extended family. And, just like those that had come before me and had paved the way for the betterment of their posterity in such a way, maybe made some substantial contribution to society, or even to the world, that they are then, remembered and maybe even hollowed. But this is what I believe; they had their time to do what they did, and now I have my time to do what I will do, and as for me and mine, I value my family greatly, and I know that, even if I'm no success to those measuring my worthiness of how I'm doing here on this earth, I'm sure that the loving, charitable, kindnesses that I offer to share to the one someone in need of nurturing and such, that act is a good seed to sow. And hopefully, I continue sew those same good seeds as a father to my children, as the patriarch to my family, as the counselor to my wife, as the neighbor down the street and as a citizen of the community.

To Thus, disowning the possessiveness of greedily encompassing worldly things, and trying to find meaning in life while passing through, that's all part of it. I thought myself in that self-same perspective and how much of my doing, of my contribution can be passed forward for others in the future. The fact is, we all have this certain amount of time that we'll be on this earth and we are all in a way, just passing through. I suppose it shouldn't matter, but there are times that I think, as my children ask in doubt, what was it that he was all about? Hopefully there's still much for me to be, and much for me to do. I still have an awful lot to learn while I'm, "*Just Passing Through?*"

Something For The Pain

(1990) - I made many attempts to put together something with these lyrics and with this concept in mind before something fell together in 1986. During that time, the Reagan years, although many people prospered and our country was in a healing mode, it was not a good time for poor people in many places, including the United States. It seemed at that time; we were a solution-less society of fish getting eaten by larger fish who in turn were being swallowed up by even larger fish. Everybody had reasons and excuses for all the problems we faced with our poor, but it seemed that there were bigger problems needing to be solved and that is where the energy was expended. The poor, and I'm not just talking about the homeless or the families living under the poverty line, but there was (and continues to be) a great disparage between the haves and the have nots. Seems so trite to use a phrase like, "the rich get richer and the poor stay poor," but since biblical times this has always been a problem. And while no one seemed to have answers or solutions to fix those problems back then, not much has changed; and, "fight the power" has come to symbolize a near impossibility make a difference. What they were getting back then is no different than what we're given today; band-aids; and that's all. And in a band-Aid society, they aren't looking to solve the problem, only cover it with something so they don't have to look at the blood, or deal with the awful hurt or the underlying the problem; instead we're semi complacent if they give us something for the pain, but as yesterday led us to today, and as today follows tomorrow, they still offer nothing for the cure.

The Day After Tomorrow

(1986) – In the mid-1980s, there was a great sellout, ravishment, and callous assault on the American farmer. Exports fell, due in part to the 1980 United States grain embargo against the Soviet Union. Farm debt for land and equipment purchases soared during the 1970s and early 1980s, doubling between 1978 and 1984. Other negative economic factors included high interest rates, high oil prices and a strong dollar. Also, the number of farms decreased from a peak of close to 7 million in the mid-1930s to just over 2 million in 1986, which led to a majority of farm household incomes coming from off-farm sources. By the mid-1980s, the crisis had reached its peak as land prices had fallen dramatically, leading to record foreclosures. The Farm Credit System experienced large losses, which were the first losses since the Great Depression.

Following in the same theme of, "Voices From The Past," the lyrics to this song reflect an apathetic societal attitude towards the farming communities, which, many of their ancestors came from. In 1986, special concerts were given by many artists like Willie Nelson and John Mellencamp, raising money for the American farmers to help them with their financial struggles, send aid to help them in that plight and their bureaucratic nightmares. I wanted to do my part, so I wrote the lyrics to this song which of course, has a lot to do with that particular American crisis.

Carried Away

(1991) - The lyrics to this song may seem to be a bit of a stretch from voices from the past, but my idea was dealing with the dysfunctionality of our society nowadays. I was having lunch one day at the Washington State Parks, in the lunchroom, with three other women and another guy. By some means, the conversation levitated to the responsibilities of raising your children. Some of the parents were frustrated and concerned that they could not relate to their teenager children. Some seemed to have given up and were even looking for the day when their teenager kids were grown-up so those problems might go away. We talked about responsibility; theirs and ours, to keep the family unit moving in a positive direction. But many of these adults that I spoke with had come to a point where they didn't want to deal with the problems anymore. And we discussed the issues of a lack of good communication where things progressively went from bad to worse, to eventual parental separations or divorces and how that impacted the kid. Someone brought up the point that, it's a shame we don't have manuals to tell us what to do in certain circumstances when something different arises and we find we suddenly have to deal with something embarrassing or difficult.

There were a lot of different opinions, but the commonality to the whole conversation was that, for many in the room, the answers boiled down to two things; protecting and cherishing the preciousness of our children, no matter what their ages are, and stepping up to our own responsibility to love the child, in spite of our own inadequacies as a parent.

Blow up the TV

(1986) - If you ever spend any time in the Baldwin House, you'll know for whom and why this song was written. Diane hates the television. Every year in the fall as school was beginning, Diane would actually hide the television somewhere in the house and then tell all the kids that they now had *one month* of no TV so that they could keep ahead of their schoolwork. Yes, kids are smart; they know there's only so many places to hide a TV in a 1000-sq.-ft. home but even when they did find where the TV was hidden, and maybe even try to put it back in place, Diane was fearless and determined, and after those kids were duly chastised for their insurrection, we went without the TV for a while.

This of course, also punished me too because I love watching college football and a lot goes on in the month of September,... But I grit my teeth and supported the woman. In her defense, it was her undying passion, (and is still to this day), to turn the TV off at any given time, for any given purpose, without any cause, other than the fact that it over-whelms a person's senses and eats up their time,.., Diane also worried about the repetitiveness of it all, especially the ongoing commercials that would indoctrinate and maybe enslave the kid's minds. And later there was a new problem; let me expound.

When I started back at JW Electronics in December of 1985, there was a guy working in the receiving area named Jerry, who was plugged in with a source to be able to get Atari 800 computers for $35.00, which included a 5 1/4-inch floppy disk drive and also with the promise that he had a large collection of software he would copy so we could use them with the computer. I jumped in right away and purchased the set.

At JW, I noticed a used, 13-inch Toshiba monitor in the back room and asked my supervisor, Jim how much he'd sell it to me for. Jim reported that the TV, (monitor) was not for sale because it had been for a product display the year earlier, but then told me to go ahead and take it home. I hooked it up in the boy's room, which, at that time, was half of the garage. In the garage I laid down some old shag carpet someone was throwing away and then put two sets of bunk beds in there and also put a mattress under one of the bunkbeds to act as a trundle bed. This allowed me to have Chet, Ben, Stephen and Spencer all in the same room. They did in fact, love it. Anyway, I hooked up the monitor in the boy's room and ran the monitor through the back of a VHS machine and hooked up a two-way switch to it so the computer could also run through the VHS machine.

Chet, who at the time was 10, fell madly in love with the whole deal and became the master and guardian to the whole system. Lori, 12, Liz, 8, and Meridith, 6, at first all seemed disinterested in the computer until Chet made the mistake of showing Lori some of the cool games they could play.

Then, Lori was on board. Ben was only four, but after watching Chet, he grasped how to turn it on, how to load a game and how to use the joystick. And Stephen, 2, got involved not too long later when he turned three or four, followed by Spencer John just a few years after that.

But I too began to question the usefulness of it all after seeing the draw the system, and especially the computer where the machine hypnotized its followers and worse, caused a kind of rebellious spirit amongst the kids wanting control over the system, and then there was the kids verses the adults where limitations and time curfews were constantly being modified or ignored. After a while, I began to think, maybe the introduction and constant never-ending influence of the mass media thing we called the TV had more than one side; and maybe one of those sides could be dark and foreboding, with altered attitudes and chronic semantics to justify bad behavior, and, maybe the TV created more problems than it solved.

And it is because I too have my moments where I have to agree with Diane's perspective or point of view, and there were times that I would also want to turn the big kaleidoscopic, omnipotent eye off, regardless of whether it was a TV program, a VHS tape movie or the Atari computer creating a cool environment in the boy's room. After it was noticed that the Baldwins had a computer, friends like Jerome Bingham and his brothers flocked over at the Baldwin's house, and maybe,... get a piece of Diane's homemade bread to eat while playing a computer game,... the 800 wasn't anything special compared to what we have now, but those Atari games that were created before the great Warner Brother's acquisition were great,... some of them required a bit of brain stuff but there were hundreds of games that I loved playing,... there's one in particular that had you go through these hoops or rings but there was a strategy and,... plus, this was hooked up to our VCR,... it was in that hallowed sanctuary where the kids and I would have our own festive viewing as we'd watch, 'Space Balls' or 'Annie' or cartoons,... and we had a lot of cartoons,... there's a whole other story on that,... but some of the best times we had there in the late 80s and early 90s, happened in that room in the garage,...those moments helped me get close to my kids doing the, 'Siskel & Ebert' discussions,... and I got to spend time figuring out who these kids in my life were,... and maybe to to let them hang out with their dad for a while,...

75

18 - MORE OF THE SAME

- 1993

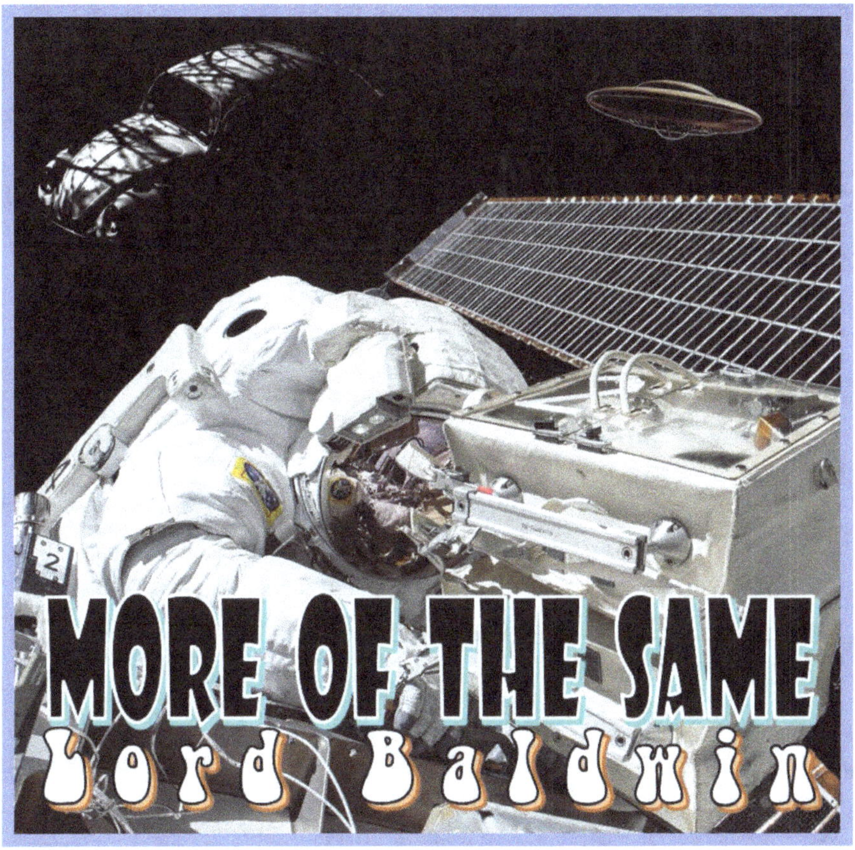

76

⚜

NOTES ABOUT THE
COVERS

Notes On The New Cover:

By this time I was taking no chances. Funny thing is, I don't even remember the artist's name that painted the front cover, I just kind of liked the kind, aloof look on the woman's face. And the city scene? Told you, I wasn't taking chances, so I created another cover.

In creating this cover, I started with a black background. Next I placed objects out in the black,... An astronaut fixing some gear out in space, but come on, even if he was changing a lightbulb, it's still a great pose, right? And then there's a part of his solar array fading into space with it's six long horizontal lines, joined with the short vertical lines give the illusion of looking down the neck of a guitar at the strings looking for a hand to reach over and form a chord. Wonder what chord that'd be? But then there's the flying saucer that has arrived to be of assistance should help be needed, and also to make sure nothing goes wrong with his fellow traveler, and we also see the space VW bug parked out in space like that's the astronaut's ride that he came to this station in and his transportation back, and we can see the shadow of a metal structure of joined pipes, above the VW Bug, and a light shining from somewhere beyond. Doesn't really have anything to do with any of the songs except "the Very," but that's good enough for me.

Notes On The Original Cover:

When I was pick for the front and back covers, I had to choose between the painting of the woman expecting someone or the city street scene by Laren's Garage with a group of kids that look like they're plotting, And some

bored kids sitting on the steps, it was a tossup of which should be on the front and which, the back. Either could

represent the songs on this al-bum, but oddly, the mood of the woman in the painting with her apprehensive, worrisome face could very well reflect many of the songs too. In the end, the painting was more mysterious and I chose it. And as you can see, still using, *Lord Chester L. Baldwin II* as my pseudonym. I'm cool with that.

77

MORE OF THE SAME

More Of The Same
One Last Chance
In My Fool's Paradise
Something Personal
The Very
I Waited Too Long
The Call Of The Road
Somebody Above And Somebody Below

78

More Of The Same

More of the same, just a different disguise,
searching for the truth through all the lies.
Meet the new boss, same as the old,
a little more callous, crafty and cold.

The classic signs come from way back when,
but it looks like we did get fooled again.
No need to point fingers at someone to blame,
it's our own fault that it's *more of the same*.

More of the same, just drawing bigger flies,
the choice is no choice and the prize is no prize.
They cry social justice, and display their cure,
while the rich get richer and the poor stay poor.

We want to relate to the words we hear
but they sound too perfect to hold so dear.
It all boils down to, who plays a better game,
then it's "Lets get down to business," to *more of the same*.

More of the same, and it never ends
like a torch passed on between sordid friends.
It's hard to know which is worse, to accept or deny,
them lying to us or us letting them lie.

It's all such an art, how can we relate
while we're so caught up that we can't see our fate?
We're drawn down the path by a face and a name,
promising the moon but giving *more of the same*.

79

One Last Chance

It must have all started when you were young,
wanting to find your one, true love.
To be married and passionately swept away
and live happily ever after that day.
It's plain now that love is not easily coerced
and to harbor illusions only makes matters worse.
Of fairy-tale endings, most never come true but
I'm still a romantic, and falling for you.

If I could have this one last chance, if I could sing you one last song,
if I could gaze within your eyes you'd see
my love is burning strong.
All of this closeness we might share, if you could know it's all real,
if I could hold you in my arms tonight,
you'd know just how I feel.

He seemed to be nice so how could you know,
he'd take what he wanted and quietly go?
He slipped into darkness with his outlaw's theft
while you lost and empty, like there's nothing left.

Shut away from love or any further abuse,
Shattered, you live the life of a lonely recluse.
Of Fairy-tale endings, most never do come true
but I'm a knight in shining armor and waiting for you.

If I could have this one last chance, if I could sing you one last song,
if I could gaze within your eyes, you'd see
my love is burning strong.
All of this closeness we might share, if you could know it's all real,
if I could hold you in my arms tonight,
you'd know just how I feel.

80

In My Fool's Paradise

When the kids left home we were all alone,
depression must have set us on separate teams.
I got it in my head that our love was dead,
and I needed to chase those lost dreams.
The more I strayed along, the more I saw the wrong,
from all the changes, I felt lost and pall.
Now I think of all we had, I want you back so bad,
I know my folly led to my downfall.

In my fool's paradise, everything was nice.
All that mattered was having a good time.
But when I opened up my eyes, I could see the lies,
and the truth is, I need you back into my life,
forever, and for always
as my wife.

As I passed from day to day, all the reasons fell away
for my leaving you alone, way back then.
So I'm looking back to see if you might consider me
to come back and be a part of you again.

There's a burning deep inside, drawing me close to your side,
though I know a price for what I did is due.
I want you to forgive all the things I said and did,
but I understand if you might refuse.

In my fool's paradise, everything was right.
The ends justified the means for all the strife.
But when I woke from all I hid, I realized what I did,
and the truth is, I need you back into my life,
forever, and for always
as my wife.

81

Something Personal

Something personal in their ways,
reaching out to fill the spaces of their days.
A close talk shared to find and draw near,
the soft concerns and dealing with the fears.

They could have chose to live their separate lives,
together, alone, with nothing shared inside.
But the caring is why both of them stays,
there's something personal in their ways.

Something personal in their lives,
A knowing trust that burns from loving eyes.
If a problem gone too far gets in the way,
they work it out and learn from their mistakes.
With commitments and concerns of what they know,
they sacrifice in hopes that love might grow.
Hard to notice any change as it arrives,
something personal in their lives.

Something personal in their love

and a closeness in the night to dream of.
What happens with a love like that in time?
They seem to strengthen bonds as years go by.
A firm trust in the other's cause and route,
to believe in each other without doubt.
The measure of their life is never done,
something personal in their love.

Something personal deep inside-
they both know that it's right.
And the cause that they pursue, carries them on,
through their lives through, on and on.

Something personal in their ways,
reaching out to fill the spaces of their days.
If a problem gone too far gets in the way,
they work it out and learn from their mistakes.
A firm trust in the other's cause and route,
they believe in each other without doubt.
Hard to notice any change as it arrives,
but there's something personal in their lives.

82

The Very

When I was young and very, I lived for summer's call.
I biked the roads and swam the holes
and tried to do it all.
As winter follows autumn, the snow stayed cold and blue.
I'd wait and yearn for spring's return
while passing on through school.
And every year it happened, I'd plot the very route,
and chase the day running each way before it all ran out.
Year by year it happened, the very all got spent.
Reflecting back, I still lost track
and wondered where it went.
Yet dreams and plans are fleeting like seasons passing by.
We take our place within the race
and leave very behind.
And now, gazing from my window, my children play their games.
I see their sweet, innocent feet
running the very ways.
And I believe the very is still within me too.
I touch a part of my child's heart,
and I'm young and very new.

83

I Waited Too Long

Heartbroken,
shaking my head,
me alone, you with him instead.
Soft spoken,
too shy to speak out,
taking my time and nursing my doubt.
Commitments,
a word or a sign,
I just couldn't step over that line.
Conditions
got out of control,
I can think why, but I'll never know.

I waited too long for the courage to come,
and to say the words
to express my love.
Afraid of rejection, or things coming out wrong,
till it was all too late,
I waited too long.

Meditating
out on the lawn,
finding purpose
now that you're gone.
I'm relating
to your side of the game,
I know I have no one else to blame.

Heartbroken
you're not in my life
looking back;
so hard to know why
Words spoken
return to me again,
It hurts to know
what might have been.

I waited too long for the courage to come,
and say the words
to express my love.
Afraid of rejection, or things coming out wrong,
till it was all too late,
I waited too long.

84

The Call Of The Road

Working too much overtime, executive on his way.
wondering why it was that I stayed on there anyway.
I got tired of the stress, that dog and pony show,
so I left it all behind
with the call of the road, and I had to go.

I weighed out everything, searched alternatives and found
there wasn't any sense in the way things all went down.
All the responsibilities were such a heavy load.
I gave up and gave in
to the call of the road and I have to go.

Like a wolf call in the night that stirs the very soul,
I dropped everything and ran to the call of the road.

Drifting like a gypsy out to see and learn.
Not concerned with politics or how the world turns.
No one may understand or approve in where I go,
but I'm happy as I travel
to the call of the road, and I have to go.

85

Somebody Above and Somebody Below

Water rolls downhill and fault becomes unfair.
People pass the buck and point fingers everywhere.
Your direction, my direction, you know how blame can go,
when there's somebody above and somebody below.
Can't deal with the conflict so they pass the bad along.
Let anybody else be responsible for the wrong.
The wisdom in it all as you're caught within it's flow
there's somebody above and somebody below.
Here it comes to you, so you pass it around the bend,
but with who or where or when will it finally end?
Going down the ladder to claim some other Joe,
you know that somebody above or somebody below.
It's water under the bridge, but your silence can still be a lie.
As you turn your head as the questions start to fly.
Sad to think a friend or even someone you don't know
is that somebody above or somebody below.
Somebody above and somebody below.

86

MEMOIRS & NOTES - 18 - 'MORE OF THE SAME'

More Of The Same

(1992) – In with the new and out with the old may not mean very much when it comes to politics and motivation of power and money, but it should. Originally written in 1992, the words to this poem originally reflected my feelings of depression and sadness that continued to haunt me after Christopher Michael's death. I just couldn't shake this sadness that fell over me and a lot of my writing was influenced by that sadness. One night, I was playing the original tune along with the dismal disheartening poem, I realized that it was too morbid even for me in my circumstances, and so I destroyed it.

Okay, So I rewrote this poem; *"More Of The Same."* to allow it to take on new direction that reflected on how the United States had gone wrong from Nixon, (Republican), who under a cloud of wrongdoing, kept us in a war to benefit big businesses and with his attempt to burglarize the Democratic National Headquarters then obstructing

Anti-Vietnam-War Demonstration

the investigation, then to Ford, (Republican), who, under the guise of healing the nation, struck a "corrupt bargain" where Ford's pardon was granted in exchange for Nixon's resignation, elevating Ford to the presidency, then to Reagan, (Republican), who, to again benefit big businesses, supplied weapons to America's enemies and armed Saddam Hussein's Iraq during the Iran-Iraq war, killing hundreds of civilians, then to George H. W. Bush (Republican), who ran a racist election campaign, (remember the Willie Horton ad?) he propagated a racist drug war, he committed war crimes dropping a 88,500 tons of bombs on Iraq and Iraqi-occupied Kuwait, responsible for thousands of civilian deaths and U.S. bombs also destroyed essential Iraqi civilian infrastructure to create postwar leverage over Iraq with intent to destroy valuable facilities that Baghdad could not repair without foreign assistance, then to Clinton, who promised to be better, (Democrat), but with the Waco Texas fiasco where federal law enforcement officers destroy the cult's compound and kill at least seventy-five people, many women and children; it was not better. So I wrote this poem; "More Of The Same" to breathe life into and give a human face to what the presidency has become.

Side Note:

As mentioned before, this song was well received by many of my family and friends, being timely to the political under-towing of the current happenings. An unfortunate side affect and later ramification to this success was that one of my motivating and driving forces to my creativity as well as one of my best critics, my brother Ray, loved this song and became so entrenched with its musical mechanics, so enthralled with its statement through its political lyrics and so con-vinced this song heralded in my finest hour, he would listen to nothing else. And so it was, I tried to get him to hear other ideas, but from here, nothing else mattered. This was a decided turning point for me because I was influenced greatly by his opinion and now this source of stimulation, inspiration, encouragement and motivation was gone.

One Last Chance

(1987) - A year before I wrote this tune, I read about Marlene Dietrich, who had shut herself up in her

apartment, refusing to social-ize or see anyone but her family. I was intrigued by the whole aspect of her fall from fame. Later in her life, in her seventies, problems with her legs, complicated with other health concerns, a broken relationship and an obsessive van-

ity, led her to totally withdraw from the public's view. In the end, a sad recluse,

alcoholic, and prisoner of her own legend, Marlene Dietrich died in Paris at her Avenue Montaigne apartment in 1992. I really loved the dark music gradually letting way to the up-tempo beat kind of like hope. And I wanted this to be someone like me coming to Marlene's rescue and assuring her that things could be wonderful for her if she could only trust one more time, trust in me.

In My Fool's Paradise

(1983) - This was one of the comeback kid songs that I wrote while at the funeral home. A realization of making a mistake and a plea for a second chance. I did some arrangements for a family who had lost a loved one during the time of separation and pending divorce. This couple originally came in together but then realized they were both still angry at each other and I found myself torn between what he wanted and what she wanted. It was a mess. This was a case of an age-old problem of possible midlife crisis on both their parts, but particularly on his. On the day that she was supposed to come to pick up the ashes, he showed up instead, at least an hour late, and in the interim we talked about this particular problem. Apparently as his kids got older, he seemed to feel less connected to his wife and kids. After the children had all left home, he figured it must be time to do something else because he felt that she, his wife, had made signs or indications that their relationship was over. He told me that he started acting like a jerk probably in hopes to have relationship dissolve more quickly. It wasn't until he had severed the ties with her and moved on that he realized his love for her. From that moment of realization, he became determined to put whatever he had broken, back together again. It's funny when you try to document happenings in people's lives that you don't even know, and develop those ideas into songs that will never be heard by anyone in particular, most specifically the people the song was written for, but at the time, it felt like the right thing to do.

Something Personal

(1991) - Originally this song was kind of a part two portion of contrasting ideas for song topics that came to me years before I finally wrote this in 1991. The two ideas stemmed originally from the idea of a song called, "nothing personal" where, after an analysis of their relationship someone realizes that they drifted apart and that their relationship is now reduced to nothing personal. Was kind of a negative thing, and to be fair with you, I wasn't as turned on to the idea of doing this song as much as I was following through with its antecedent, "Something Personal."

It is my ongoing hope to figure out what it is that makes our relationship so special. I wanted to document just what it is that makes our love so special. In a truer sense, I evaluated our relationship and found some interesting facts, basic principles, shared ideas, possible flaws, ongoing problems, and in general the main philosophies and internal glues if you will, that have helped to cement and keep our relationship together for so long.

Side Note:

this song is the first of five songs in a row that eventually finish this album, all of them written in 1991. I don't know how this happened, it was too long ago for me to remember, but maybe I just happened to be in that particular book of songs from 1991 and I just recorded them as such,... I don't think so.

Second Side Note:

this song has a little ditty to it that is woven through the beginning, middle and the ending that, I'm not sure how to put this, but to me, the little woven tune with a chord structure that goes from tonic to subdominant, kind of carries a little message that could be a sense of hope and solid determination with a possible reward of a shared future. After I recorded this song, this little 10-second prelude tune kept haunting me to the point where, like Alfred Hitchcock doing a cameo appearance in his own movies, I have included this interwoven tune somewhere in just about all of my albums that have followed.

The Very

(1991) - Returning to that yesteryear when I had the magic and joy of innocence and youth. In the fall of 1991 Allison was not quite one, Christopher was three years old, Spencer was five, Stephen was 8, Ben was 10, Meredith was 12, Elizabeth was 14, Chet was 16, and Lori was still 17. There is a lot of magic going on at the time in the Baldwin House and it was my hope to try to document that magic as best as I could into this song. It all began with me watching Spencer, Christopher, Stephen, and Ben playing out in the front yard. I don't remember what game they were playing or what they were pretending to be at the time, but I can still remember Spencer coming into the house and inviting me to join them in play. I went out for a while, and I remember how impressed I was with their elaborate thought process while constructing this small temporary universe they were all in. After a short while I have to admit I got drawn out of play by other responsibilities like school and work. That kind of special moment where I was included and involved in wonderful play, pretending right along with the four of my youngest boys was an incredible experience, and yet, due to many extenuating circumstances, never happened again. Afterwards I was back in the living room looking out the window at the boys still in play.

Back Row: John, Jack, Ed, David - Front Row: Ray, Richie & Me

Side Note:

With regards to the enigmatic analogy of "The Very" itself, in some respects I worry that I did not completely capture the full essence of the innocent, naïveté simplicity of being a kid, leastwise, not quite what I envisioned in my mind, but with the tune and the timing that went with the words, and that harmonica? I came dangerously close.

I Waited Too Long

(1991) - You know, this was another one of those songs where I was sitting on the bed banging on the guitar and hoping something might shake out of it.

Returning to that yesteryear, when I had the magic and joy of innocence and youth,... as with many songs, the chorus became solid first and the rest of the song followed. Some of you that read this may relate to the fact that sometimes you creatively put something together, it all sounds good, and you think you might really have some-thing with potential,... something that might possibly take you out of the unchanged situation that you've been into for so long,... and at one time this song seemed like that to me,... but I moved on,... and years later I revisited the song only to find it took on an uneasiness to the piece,... and I was not looking for a kind of commonality with much of my other works,... I wanted the emotions in my voice to speak out of the heart of the poem itself,...

Side Note:

There are times that I wonder if I was that one that has waited too long to get in the music business; that dream I have chased my whole life. Part of me morns for the chances at fame and fortune that never arrived, and for the lost opportunities to perform on stage, or to be recognized for my accomplishments, and to have a validation for

the work I do as the musician and poet. But I may be the only one to know it, but I still believe myself to be unique and I will continue to press on, creating and recording those little songs that keep popping up in my head, always waiting here on the edge; on the outside of the music industry, looking in.

Another Side Note:

I want all of you folks out there reading this side note, to know that I did have choices to make, and when those music opportunities came knocking on my door, (and there were times that it did), I couldn't, in good conscience, answer that door. I felt, during those "golden opportunity" times, as I do to this day; my family always comes first. Oh, I've been tempted at times to maybe rationalize, "the ends justifying the means" argument, but I was always able to peek into the door and see I had more important things to do. And when those chances came around, it seemed I was always in the middle of something else going on, (usually family related), that if I was to turn my mind away from, and get out there to get noticed, it always seemed to come at a time where, if I shifted my

Open Mike 1992 - SPSCC

attention away from my family, my kids and/or my wife would have suffered by my leaving. My staying back to be in charge my little command always took priority; the family, always the most important. And I figured that the right time may come for me to spread my wings and get out there. And when or if that ever happens, it will probably be after the kids have grown up. That won't prevent me from pressing on or writing new poetry, (lyrics), and putting my brand of music to that material to create something special. And, because of my little dream on hold, there will probably be more times where I still lament the personal dilemma, I'm in, and there will probably be more songs down the road that will document those lamentations, but such is the life of the unknown songwriter, and I say, so be it.

Yet Another Side Note:

I know that I have been greatly blessed with the opportunity to be a husband to my wonderful Diane and a father to all my amazing kids. Could there be anything more precious or valuable than my family?

And if I die tomorrow, the question I would ask myself is, "How'd you do?" And I just know that that question would not be centered on anything but my family. My other thoughts about how I spent my other time would not be important anymore to me or the Lord. But it doesn't stop there, my friend. I know the Lord knows of me. He's watching me making my choices; some good, some, not so good, but I'm thankful as I report that He's given me a unique but extraordinary gift for me to combine with the music in my heart, to be able to continue to express myself with my unusual but original, "*In-House Jazz*" creations, and I gotta say, a big thanks again for that gift,... thanks again.

The Call Of The Road

(1991) - There was this guy named Mike Giovanni who used the phrase, "Dog And Pony Show" referring to a meeting that he was going to have to go to the following week. I never heard that phrase and inquired what it meant and when Mike told me, I was intrigued by its connotation.

I built the whole song around and about an individual who had gotten fed up with his circumstances and left the corporate world for the big wide-open spaces of freedom. Interestingly, maybe three years later, I met someone that was involved with the Education and Training Development Program at South Puget Sound Community College who was in fact an up-and-coming executive on his way that left the business and stress, bought a mobile home and decided to travel across the United States, mostly to see the New England States. I believe he is passing through Delaware even as we speak. Doing what you do for a good reason. Doing "it" for you. Oh, and good harmonica at the end.

Somebody Above, Somebody Below

(1991) - After working at the Washington State Parks and Recreation Department for just a short while, I learned this principle very well.

This was especially relevant due to the fact that for a long while, because I was the last man in and there wasn't any other person below me, I was faced with everyone else's problems and things usually became my fault. But after a while even for me, there was somebody above and somebody below. Accepting or to be sure, not accepting responsibility.

Side Note:

I loved the blending of three musical entry each wanting to lead. The organ music on this one is fun. I had just landed on the setting and used it here. And it's not the only place beyond. There's this harmony with me, that is me, that sounded like they were goofing on each other.

At The End

(1991) – (Instrumental) Before we go, just a few words on the musical piece, "**At The End**." This was a big leap for me, creating longhair music. With my Yamaha PRS-500 keyboard, I was now experimenting with sounds and voices and mixing things together in different combinations, all in hopes of making something new and different, like this here cool, **In-House Jazz** piece. It was lots of fun experimenting with the new voices.

Side Note:

Speaking about "**At The End**," armed with the *Yamaha PRS-500 keyboard*, I decided to stop worrying about how others perceived my newer musical compositions, many with succinct time constraints,... and instead, I began to lengthen the preludes and postludes of my songs with more free-style instrumentations and experimental sounds. This change and new freedom was rather cathartic for me, especially with the realization that this new style was much more logical to my brain that felt I was cheating the listener by hurrying up the beginnings and the conclusions,... and overall, the pieces became more mathematically sound.

From here on out, I recorded the songs from how and where the music would take me and if I ended up with only seven songs instead of eight or nine, that was okay. I wanted my own unrestrained frame of mind to be able to dictate the beginnings and endings as well as maybe more content in the poetry,... it was liberating.

87

- 19 - EXPECTING RAIN

NOTES ABOUT THE COVERS

Notes On The Original Cover:

Okay, okay. Yes I could have recycled these covers, (front & Back), and I do love me this 1950s Panel truck, but neither had enough appeal in this day and age, as far as I'm concerned. In fact, I originally wanted to use a heavy gray cloud, but it didn't look

ominous enough. So the lightning won out for the front cover, and the panel for the back cover.

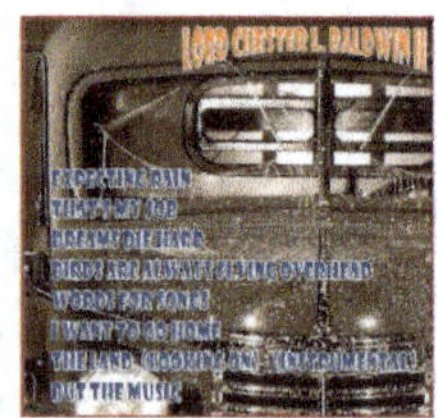

Note On The New Cover:

Originally, before I started scanning the web for cover ideas, back in 1995, (which is when the college got the internet and Andrew Poltridge and Ray Dooly installed networking for it in my computer lab that summer), my idea was to have a picture of me out in the weather with an umbrella, holding my hand out to see if it was raining. Long before smart phones, didn't have a digital camera, nor do I think I could have done anything with Windows 3.1, and this album was just one of 45 albums that needed covers.

The photo of the new album was taken by Diane,... and yes, that is me in one of my Camp Parsons Boy Scout tee shirts, out in the (sunny) weather with an umbrella, and I'm holding out my hand to see if it's raining. It was just what I wanted, only a few years late,... but, I was happy to finally get the cover close to my original idea.

89

EXPECTING RAIN

Expecting Rain
That's My Job
Dreams Die Hard
Birds Are Always Flying Overhead
Words For Songs
I Want To Go Home
But The Music

90

Expecting Rain

She lied to me, and I took the bait,
and found out the truth when it was far too late.
Wheels were in motion, things started to fall,
while I was there trapped in the middle of it all.
I loved that girl, as the one I'd keep,
no big surprise that I fell in so deep.
Looking back, I guess I'd do it all again,
even with the gray clouds and expecting rain.

Expecting rain, I'm ready to get wet,
I'm waiting to find out how deep I am in debt.
Love always involves some joy and pain,
and I'll ponder that thought while expecting rain.
Yeah, expecting rain;
I'm expecting rain.

She lied to me, but I disregarded the rest,
I guess I just wanted to believe the best.
But sooner or later, the little lies fell apart,
and the truth hit me hard like a bullet to my heart.

I loved that girl, and I wanted to believe,
so when I found out about him it devastated me.
Looking back, I know I should have left on that train,
I'd be miles from here and not expecting rain.

Expecting rain, I'm ready to get wet,
as I wait to find out how deep I am in debt.
Love always involves some joy and some pain,
and I'll ponder that thought while expecting rain.
Yeah, I'm expecting rain. I know,
I'm expecting rain.
Got my umbrella ready,
cause I'm expecting rain.

91

That's My Job

Turn off the lights that someone's left on,
stop the flow of water that's flooding the lawn.
I fix what is broke, do maintenance checks,
and call in the cavalry when I'm in over my head.
My attitude sways, I may mutter to the breeze,
still, I know there's people
depending on me.

That's my job that God gave to me,
that's my job, and I take it seriously.
For the rest of my life, I will carry this through,
that's my job; it's what I do.

All broken toys and appliances get sent here to me.
I fix broken hearts and mend their broken dreams.
I'm a carpenter, a plumber, a laborer for life,
I'm a teacher to my kids and a counselor to my wife.
I try not to be too busy for all the little things
like feelings and concerns that each new day brings.

That's my job that God gave to me;
that's my job; I take it seriously.
For the rest of my life, I will carry it all through,
that's my job; it's what I do.

As evening comes on, and I'm tired and spent
from the long hard day and the way things went,
I think of my life, compared with great men
and find myself questioning my place from all that I have been.
Still, as children call me to join them within,
it takes shape
as their love comes pouring in.

That's my job, that God gave this to me;
that's my job and I take it seriously.
For the rest of my life, I will carry this through,
that's my job, it's what I do.

92

Dreams Die Hard

Make it all last, help us get past
the hard times we're going through now.
All that we see; all the things that we need
tomorrow won't matter anyhow.

Make it all due, Honey help us get through
the long days that never seem to end.
I know things are wrong, but Darling, we can be strong
hand in hand we face everything with a friend.

Dreams die hard as we leave behind
the things we can't use anymore.
But as we pass through these trials and errors
we stand at the threshold of another door.

Make it all due, Honey help us get through
the hard days that follow us here.
Although things are rough, Darling, we can be tough
and not give into desperation or fear.

Dreams die hard so it's easy to lose
perspectives, where we've been, and where we are.
But as the resentment of everything passes
looking back, we can see that we've come real far.

So, make it all last, Honey help us get past
the hard times we're going through now.
And all that we seek, all the things we thought we'd need
tomorrow won't matter anyhow.

93

Birds Are Always Flying Overhead

Birds are always flying overhead;
they call to me as they wing their way.
I've no wings to touch the clouds they shed
and so I wait for another day.

Shoes with holes let in the rain and snow,
but I make due, with no place left to go.
Somehow all these years and time went by;
here am I, somewhere in my life.
I didn't plan to fail, I only failed to plan.
My situation changed,
now I'm a broken man.

Birds are always flying overhead;
they call to me as they wing their way.
I've no wings to soar the skies they tread,
and I must wait
while the sun moves through the day.

Dreams with holes are fragile like thin glass,
they shatter easily and time goes by so fast.
Seems like when we least expect a change,
things fall apart, and we're left out of range.
In the shadow of their wings,
I raise my head to see,
forms moving with direction
off and away from me.

Birds are always flying overhead;
they look down to me
as they wing their way.
I've no wings to fly the sunset red,
I can only watch
as they fly away.

Birds are always flying overhead;
they call to me
as they wing their way.
I've no wings to touch the clouds they tread
and so I wait
for my big day.

94

Words For Songs

The words for songs fall short, it's true with all I try to say to you.
Words could never represent the feelings of the love I meant.
The meanings sometimes falls apart,
and can't reflect the special heart.
I only hope sometimes I say how much you mean to me each day.

Words for songs that flow to rhyme and try but fail to say my mind
Words for songs to draw us near and wait for you to hear.

The words for songs fall short and miss
and how can I come close to this?
The words could never represent the feelings of this love I've spend.
Though the meanings sometimes fall and reflects part but never all.
I only hope sometime, some way,
you'll know from my words, what I say.

Words for songs that flow to rhyme
and rarely reflect my true mind.
Words for songs to draw us near and wait for you to hear; to hear.

95

I Want To Go Home

So far away from all I know and love.
The distance only makes it harder to think of.
I get letters at times but they're never enough
to replace the pain that grows more with every day.
Lost and alone in such a distant place,
thinking back of home and everybody's face.
I try to lose myself in the job's quick pace,
but a hunger burns and all of this loneliness returns.
I want to go home, I wanna go home, I need to go home.
I want to go home, I need to go home, I wanna go home.
The time goes slowly, from each day to day.
keep working towards the time that I will get away.
I wonder if its all worth this price that I pay.
And all this emptiness inside that stays with me every night.
If I could be back to see all of them right now,
I'd see my friends at the hangout in town.
My Family's together, but not complete with me out,
and I just know I'd see they're saving a place for me.
I want to go home, I need to go home, I wanna go home.

96

But The Music

Again, it calls to me in the quiet of the night.
Just like the still small voice declaring what is right.
This like a secret no one ever hears or sees,
this one creation is alive and part of me.
And it soothes my soul with no charge or toll,
I am in control; there's no need play the role today.
Play the music, helps my heart to fly away.

But the music, the music is my life,
and maybe in my time I may yet see it shine.
All this music; the music is my way, to end a turmoil day
and cast my cares away.

I see the music join, a story then to tell.
Just like the sculpture who knows his work's done well.
I thank the Lord for inspiration; I've been blessed.
All things from there will find a purpose for all the rest.
And the sounds set free are a symphony
to give liberally to all hearts in need of peace.
To set the mind at ease, and for all this, I succeed.

With my music; hey there's music in my life,
and maybe in my time I may yet see it shine.
All the music; the music will go on,
and even when I'm gone, someone else might sing along.
Sing the melody as a part of me; echoes wild and free
for eternity of time. And if the words don't rhyme,
who cares, if you're feeling fine.

But the music; the music is my life, and maybe in my time
I may yet see it shine.
All the music; the music is my way
to help my turmoiled day,
and to cast my cares away.

Again, it calls to me in the quiet of the night.
Just like that still small voice declaring that it's time.
I may seem lost at moments; so far away,
but I am my music as it transcends on its way.

But the music; the music is my life, and maybe in my time
I may yet see it shine.
All the music, the music will go on,
and even when I'm gone,
someone else will sing along.

97

MEMOIRS & NOTES - 19 - 'EXPECTING RAIN'

Expecting Rain

(1992) – In the spring of 1992 I was once again unemployed. One day I was down at the Washington

state unemployment office and met one of my friends (Ralph), that I had gone to school with. He told me that he had heard that there were a few openings at the Western State Hospital up in Tacoma. We both made arrange-

ments and applied for the job and we both got interviews the same day so we drove up together. When we got there, I parked the car and when we went inside, we saw another one of our fellow graduated friends, (Randy), who gave as an unofficial tour of the facilities. We went in for my interview and I went before a panel of people that asked some qualifying questions followed by special questions dealing with mentally ill patients and ended the interview with pleasant conversations about

287

other things. Two of the interviewers, a tall man of 30 and a short man of maybe 25, held me up for a moment and the taller one began talking about my interests and extracurricular activities, (music). Looking between them both I told them that I was indeed a songwriter.

This intrigued the shorter one, who looked to his partner before saying, "We're songwriters too." Then he looked to his partner again before saying, "Yeah, and we're working on a song right now, but we're stumped right now."

"I could help you with the song if you'd like." I replied.

"Really?"

"Sure, I'd be glad to. So, do you have it typed up or something?"

"yeah," The shorter man replied, "got it on this sticky note." He then pulled out the small yellow piece of paper and trading from it, said, "She lied to me."

That's it?" I asked, waiting for more of the verse.

He nodded,...

"That's all you have?" I asked, thinking they were goofing on me.

"Yeah so far." shorter man replied, smiling like it was already the best thing I'd ever heard.

"Okay," I said, "What's it about?"

"It's like, the realization that she lied to him," The shorter man replied, glancing over at his taller friend for approval before continuing, "and he believed her, but then he finds out that love is not what it was hoped to be, and realizes that the relationship may be about to change, and probably not for the better."

"Okay." I replied, smiling. "The next time I come up here I have it."

I should share with you that prior to the conversation about the song, after they had finished their interviewing process, I was told that they were impressed with my credentials, and that they shouldn't tell me this, but, then one of them looked around the room before saying excitedly but with a rather soft-spoken voice, "You got the job."

This of course made me feel good and I went home to celebrate with Diane. But that confirming phone call that was supposed to come Monday morning, didn't happen. Nor did it happen Monday night or for the rest of that week, and for that matter, I never got a call from Western State Hospital at all. I called them back, thinking my contact information was wrong, but their human resource department would only tell me that they were still in the hiring process, and confirm that the contact information that they had on file was correct.

Meanwhile I had written the first four lines to the poem and had already started composing the second stanza, and I was kind of digging it. Then, maybe three weeks later, a letter came in the mail informing me that another candidate was stronger in her skills and that they hired her. A Couple of weeks later, I saw Randy at the Mega Foods grocery store in Tumwater, and he told me that that the Western State Hospital computer department had hired the girl from Spokane, because they had to follow affirmative action rules and regulations. He also said that this person was not working out and that they would really like for me to resubmit my application. I told him to tell them that I would not resubmit my application, but that in fact, I no longer wanted to work there. Meanwhile by now I had the words to the poem done and the chords to the music sketched out, but the wind was out of my sails, and the song was a reminder of one of my lost opportunities, so it got buried in my paperwork somewhere and did not resurface or get consideration for being recorded until later.

Side Note:

As mentioned in my last album, it was my hope to impress my brother Raymond with this album, especially due to the fact that he was so preoccupied with the song, "More Of The Same." I even made a special trip down to Oregon to present this album and have him listen to it, but it was to no avail and the words and the music and my efforts all seemed to fall on deaf ears and Ray's pseudo-friend, John Cameron was only mildly interested.

Another Side Note:

While I was still in Canby visiting, I ventured down under Ray's house to see the basement that Ray and his kids had dug out. They had put carpet remnants on the dirt and had a couch down there to make things

Ray's House in Canby

comfortable. When I arrived down there, I met this guy sitting on the couch drinking a quart of beer. His name was Mike Wilson and we became good friends after I told him I was a songwriter. When I played this song for him, he was flabbergasted. Later that evening Ray was driving us to his Code One with Mike in the passenger seat and me in the back with my guitar. I played "*Blue With A Broken Heart*" and Mike couldn't believe I had written the song. Then, one song after another, (it's a long ride to Code One) Mike would continue to say things like, "Well, that's a hit" and, "Million-dollar song" and "No, really? You wrote that?" From that day forward, we were good friends and Mike would always seem to be at Rays place when I came down. And I have to admit, it was swell on my ego and motivated me to continue writing songs.

That's My Job

(1992-93) – from the beginning of all of my songwriting I could categorize everything into a couple of boxes; like, love songs, and by love songs I could mean positive love songs that I wrote for Diane, or the many negative, "love gone bad" type of songs, or political songs dealing with the problems and complications of today's society, or songs like this one, which I categorize as a family song. I may have mentioned in the past that I'm a family man, and the words to this song are an affirmation and a proud declaration of my acceptance to this exalted calling. And out of all of the family songs that I have written, this is definitely one of my favorites. It was my hope to epitomize my position as the father, the husband, and the homemaker, and by homemaker, I mean the person designated to fix whatever is broken or to indeed mend whatever problem is put in front of me. Sometimes the words and music come together in just a way that I have to say, "yeah, man!" This was one of those songs.

Side Note:

Imagine a double bed situated under the bedroom window and to the left and right of the bed was five-gallon buckets filled with food storage, (in this case, we had Montana wheat or honey, the buckets spaced out with boards horizontally going across to make openings that we used as shelving. I slept on the left side and used the shelf space

to put my TASCAM Cassette Recorder and in the 26-inch space between the shelf and the bed was my recording space. I would stand and sing into my Shure 55s microphone situated next to the wall by the window or I would sit on the bed with my guitar, giving me just enough space to record in. Not ideal accommodations, but it was what I had to work with and I was too excited with the prospect of being able to be recording to care; I just dealt with it. This in-

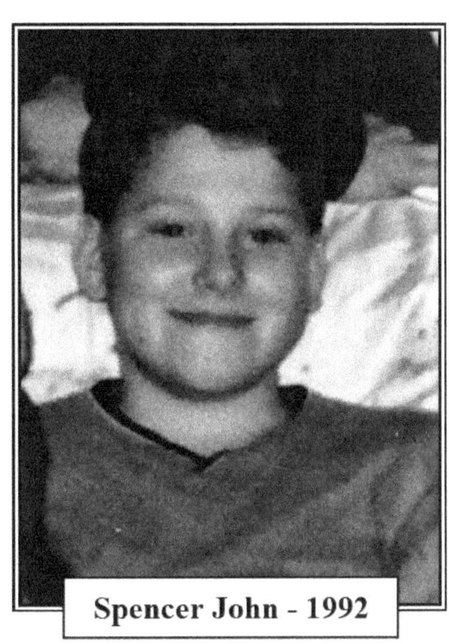

Spencer John - 1992

formation is important to note as I elaborate why.

At the end of this song, you can hear some little kid laughing. That was Spencer. It was not unusual for Spencer, probably six or seven at the time, to come find me and bug me; he was always a kid that liked to interact with me when I was home during the day, and at the time, especially because it was in the middle of the day on a Saturday or Sunday, he knew I was supposed to be focused somewhere else other than my bedroom, recording a song. Diane was over visiting next door but the kids all seemed preoccupied, so, excited that I had laid down most of the tracks to this song, I was ready to put the vocals to it. So, I shut the door and stepped into my bedroom's recording space and got all the equipment ready. I no sooner got started, with a wave of cool harmonica, before the door swings open and spencer comes in and walks up to me talking like nothing is happening. I raise my finger as if to say, give me one minute, knowing that this was over five minutes long, hoping he would give me a little space. But if you listen carefully, he can be heard starting to say something just before I gave him the stink eye, which quieted him but did not leave. He was very patient; at least for a kid with Attention Deficit Disorder he was patient. I picked up my harmonica, getting ready for the finale, and I and motioned to him, as I raised my, "I'm-almost-done" pointer finger up, to indicate that I was almost done; all the while, I was hoping to finish singing the last verse. But the song as a whole had already gone too long, and Spencer couldn't stand waiting anymore. He climbed on the bed and got right next to me and started talking, so I reached over and tickled him to buy me just those last few moments I needed to get the verse out and I motioned to him with a pleading glance, "Could you please wait till the end of the song." Oh, and there's one more factor that I need to mention. All this time, except for the live, harmonica or my singing, Spencer couldn't hear what it was that I was doing because I had no monitor speakers and everything was coming through my head-phones; Spencer had no idea where I was in the song or how long the song was. But, believe it or not it, it did quiet him up... for about ten seconds before he got off the bed and stood there defiantly next to me with a big smile on his face. So with the microphone hot, I continued singing the last verse and simultaneously I started tickling him, which caused him to lean in and force me to continue tickling him for about four measures or 32 beats. Seriously, after finishing the song I realized there was no way I would take that sound byte out of the song; the spontaneity and timing was just too good to be true. And, I was really happy with the background to forefront harmonica.

Second Side Note:

Now keep in mind that the TASCAM Cassette Recorder only allows four slots for recording onto, but as I felt like I was getting better at putting my words and music down, I would experiment, putting in a different, and I mean unconventional, or unusual instrument to add and mix sound, (think, color), to the piece, (think canvas to a painting), these new, or odd, or unorthodox voices were a lot of fun, and in the process, I used the first accordion sound, (#16 Accordion 1). Although the idea of using an accordion sound appealed to me, I knew the voice was still not quite the professional sound one might want, but it quickly grew on me. I immediately felt it had a warm inviting voice that seemed to cement itself into this song. Yes, there may be other songs that I'll include an accordion, but sometimes I feel like adding the hopeful sound of an accordion to an otherwise dark shade to give the song a possible path out of the darkness, but for the most part, after *"That's My Job,"* because I liked the effect as well the vibes it had on this song so much, from this point forward, I reserved the use of the accordion sound to be included exclusively in feel-good and up-tempo songs about family, encouragement, songs from place, and songs for kids.

Third Side Note:

I need to let you know that I was already bias to the sounds of an accordion because an accordion, like a harmonica, is nothing more than a complicated reed instrument; arguably a reed instrument on steroids. And I grew up playing harmonica. I've told this story before but maybe you won't mind me repeating it.

You've already got a pretty good idea about how it was to grow up in a home with an abusive stepfather, where I was just baggage from his marriage to my mother. Christmases usually sucked, but imagine, my birthday was 19 days after Christmas; and there was the running narrative from Senior who would say "We spent so much on Christmas, we don't have any money left over." For my birthday all the time, I would get a card and a pair of socks. That all ended when I was 12. The fall of 1961 I bought a chromatic harmonica at the garage sale for a nickel. It did have a few dead reeds but I treasured that harmonica and my mother knew it. On my next birthday, I got a pair of socks and a card with a dollar in it. But later, my mother called me aside and handed me the rectangular present that turned out to be a Hohner Marine Band harmonica. It was awesome!! And every year after that, my mother continued the tradition of giving me a new harmonica for my birthday. The last birthday harmonica from her came on my 18th birthday and was a Hohner 280/64 Chromonica, 64-Reed Chromatic Harmonica. Which, I'm happy to say I played with for years until it was stolen from my Kingston Apartment days.

One Last Side Note:

(Well maybe two) -There are two reasons the accordion is so special to me; first; when I was fourteen or fifteen,

living in the Bell Acres Trailer Park in Glendora California, I found in a big, heavy buckled carrying case sitting on the back porch, but I didn't dare open it without permission. Later that evening I spoke with my mother who told me it was an accordion, and that she was holding on to it as collateral from a friend that had borrowed money from her. She said it would be holding on to it for a couple of weeks, but, she said that I could play with it, just be careful with it. Now I didn't know how to play the accordion, but that did not stop me from playing with it. From that brief interaction, (we ended up having the accordion for about a month), I figured out accountments to songs like Green Sleeves and Oh Suzanna, but most important, I learned about chord progressions and how I could play those same songs in different keys.

The second reason is that my dad plays accordion and the sound of one always brings me back home to the farm where he would not have to be coaxed for very long to break his accordion out and do a set of his favorites.

Dreams Die Hard

(1983) – Sometimes knowing which dreams are important to pursue and also important to know when to put that dream on hold or even when to let that dream go. It was Gary Rook, the Managing Funeral Director at Forest Funeral Home and Forest Memorial Gardens, who, one evening, after we had finished discussing his one-time dream of owning a 1965 Shelby Cobra, coined the phrase, "we leave behind the things we can't use any more." I was intrigued by the phrase and it stuck with me for months before I wrote this song, which is a kind of a combination between a love song and a family song.

Birds Are Always Flying Overhead

(1993) – A person sees others with control and direction over their destinies, but knowing that there is a personal need in his own life to get his act together. At the time this song was written I was now working for the South Puget Sound Community College, (SPSCC). The same college that I had graduated from a year earlier. I now had a Technical Degree in Computer Science and I was working in a rather technical position with the college, and

managing my own computer lab; yet, I still felt incomplete.

One day I was walking down the hall in Building 22, it was a time between classes where students go from one class to the other and the halls were filled with what seemed to be, bright confident people that knew where they were going, had a plan and knew what they were going to do. I kind of felt like I was on the ground and they were all above me going their way, and the thought occurred to me that these confident students were like birds winging to their known destinations while I was stuck where I was doing what I was doing and would be that way forever. As I walked to the cafeteria, the tune came to me in my head and I began to sing the words, "birds are always flying overhead." I was so impressed with the marriage of the music and the words, that I could not wait to finish this song that came out of the cafeteria, almost immediately, and I found myself staying after work that night to finish up the lyrics and then, took the finished product home and recorded the song that very night, even though I had to stay up close to three o'clock in the morning just to get it right.

Side Note: from the beginning drum beats, and then throwing in the organ; I was experimenting with different percussion accompaniments when I found this samba-like gem. The accordion was put in to soften the samba effect and then this organ sound, (#13 electronic organ 2) to carry the warm flow of music to grace my singing. There were other voices tried, but many of them would seem to say, hey, don't listen to him, listen to me. Meanwhile, I did this staccato-like, three-stroke attack on my guitar to give the song a special addition and to complete the essence of this recording.

Words For Songs

(1991) – Originally when I wrote my the songs and compiled them into folders labeled book one, book two, book 3 etc., each one had the title, "Words For Songs." In my quest to maximize my writing possibilities during my lunchtime, I thought that the term, Words For Songs could be used in the context of a love song in and of itself. I was holding the drums back until the chorus to give the chorus a surprise voice and more body, and then I'd take it off till the second chorus came around and then, re-introduce the percussion. There was also great harmonica work that carried through to the end.

Side Note:

Sometimes words are inadequate to express the feelings of the heart. When I was recording this song, I thought I might add the percussions before the first chorus began, giving it kind of an effect and breaking the monotony. Unfortunately, I forgot to turn the drumming on during the first chorus, and it wasn't until the end that I turned it on but then quickly turned it off again. But when the chorus came around again, I was ready, and I turned it on. When I was engineering the master, I reviewed and rereviewed the recording, thinking that I would probably have to edit and/or rerecord certain parts of song, I was surprised to hear that, even with the 5-second-drum blunder, all in all, I liked it; it sounded good, almost like it was planned, and so, I left it just the way it was recorded.

I Want To Go Home

(1985) –Although the database says that this song was written in 1985, I began writing this song during the spring of 1982. I was out of work, to be sure I was fired from JW Electronics, (by my brother-in-law), arguably because I was insufferable to be around the management, and I had this chance to work as a draftsman for company called Burns and Roe Construction, which was in Jacksonville Florida. Because of our financial circumstances we had little money to afford any type of career change at the time, so I left Diane and four children at home in Olympia Washington, and then flew off to Jacksonville by myself. At first things looked good when I got there and I called Diane once a week to give her a progress report and find out how things were going back home. It was not too long before everything started falling apart from both sides of the continent.

The Burns and Roe Construction Company and their promises, one by one, fell by the way, and I was left with not only less money, but a lower position in the company then originally promised, which I could have worked with, but the commitment and promise to move my family from Olympia, Washington to Jacksonville, Florida dissolved, and at that point, I was left with some tough decisions. All the while I was gone, I imagined how my family was dealing with my absence, waiting for me to come back home again, and how Diane left the light burning for me on the front porch, and in her heart.

I got a letter from the family, maybe on a weekly or biweekly basis, and in one of the letters Lori, who at the time was probably eight years old, said that there was a place setting for me at the kitchen table every night. This touched me greatly and it was from that letter and the feelings that I got through reading Lori's letter that this song was created.

Side Note:

I am not sure why it was that this song got categorized into 1985, especially after all evidence to the contrary,

but I do have a guess. I know that this song, or to be more precise, the words for this song as well as a group of songs it was included in, were all lost at one point. Even worse, some of the titles to the songs, which for sometime was the only way I knew of the song's existence, were left out of my other documentation. This was one of the songs that had never been properly documented, and even when I realized that some of my songs were missing, I was only able to recreate the majority of them that I had titles to. But I didn't even know this song was missing until I started typing all the words for songs that I had created up to that time I worked at Forest Funeral Home from 1982 to 1985.

Another Side Note:

You know, a while back I was telling you how I would write a song for a particular artist? Well, maybe not when I was writing this song, but later on, I really felt that Bonnie Raitt, with her blues style, her strong, confident voice, and her unique falsetto, well I really felt she could do justice this song. But to be fair, and at that time, Warner Brothers was not responding to any of my mail, let alone passing my mail on down the line.

The Land

(1993) – Instrumental – I was just playing with different chords when this materialized. In this experimental piece I played with at least a dozen voices in chord changes before I settle on these. In concert with the chords, I visualized an old farmer wearing an old fedora, and heavy work clothes, and standing next to him is the woman he loves, who is also dressed warm because it is an early morning winter day. They are standing on the back fence of the old farm house. The old man is looking out across the farm; the old ramshackle barn, the dilapidated equipment shed, the tumble-down cedar fence, the cows, horses and other animals, braving the weather, standing next to the gate, waiting for the barn to finally open so they can get something to eat. He gazes beyond or seemingly through the property itself and everything on it, and he smiles. He breathes in slowly realizing the rich heritage the land is to him and his family that have owned this land for six generations. He puts an arm around the woman he loves and pulls her in close, and with a small squeeze he looks into her eyes and smiles.

But The Music

(1977) – A note of thankfulness for this magnificent thing inside me that connects me and my psyche with the universe, and all because of music. It almost seems kind of self-centered or narcissistic for me to write about why I like to write, about what I like to write about, what and how I compose music, or for me to write about how good I am with what I've done here. First, let me say that I am so far from being phenomenal in any of the categories; my guitar work is, well, it's a work in progress. My keyboarding skills, while I don't read music and I can't do arpeggios very well, I still do pretty well, putting my songs together. And I love to sing my creations, but I don't believe my voice to be anything special; still, you put it all together and it has its own life.

I also want to say that, from the beginning, (and I may have mentioned this before), it was always my intention to have my songs, all my recordings, it was always supposed to be done in a recording studio, where I would be backed by professional musicians, where there would be conversations on how to make this the best album ever, with smoother recordings, with less mistakes, with all the right gear, I mean, it has always been a dream of mine to own an acoustic Gibson guitar, the one with the thinnest neck and solid wood all around, but I could never afford such a luxury of a Gibson guitar when I had a hard time making my house payments. Sorry, I got off track. Back to the recording; it was always my intention to put out that quality product after engineers and producers and all the other guys I don't even know about, but it would all come together to master my works. But that didn't happen, so I decided to just do what ever I could to create some songs and then create my own albums, and have a lot of fun with it.

One early frosty morning, where when I was washing off the cow to get her ready to be milked, and steam is rising from the cows utters (and also from the trough), I was surprised to see my dad out there that early. (After my brother Richie and I came to live on the farm, the only time my dad ever came out to the barn in the morning was Saturday or Sunday) Anyway, my dad walks back to check on the pigs and he's singing this song from a 1954 movie, "There's No Business Like Show

Business." I could hear him singing to the chickens as he went by the indoor coop. By this time, I had a half a gallon of milk but things were going slow. My dad comes over and says, "You know, if you take a towel off the back porch and get it wet with hot water, not too hot, then after you wash the utters, you take that warm, moist towel and wrap it around the hole utter, and then wait for, I don't know, minute,... maybe half a minute, you'll know because the cow will relax when she gets warmed up,... and then the milk comes out faster and she's thanking you for the hot towel, try it tomorrow and see what I mean."

I stopped milking, looked up, I asked, "How long you been playing the accordion?"

My dad thought for a moment, began to say a number but then said, "Since I was 12."

"And did you learn how to read music?"

"Oh yeah," He replied. "But I spent years learning how to read the music well enough to play the notes so the song sounds the way the composer wrote."

I went back to milking as I said, "Can I ask you a question?"

"Aren't you doing that right now?" My dad said smiling.

"Uh, what I,..." I stammered before he interrupted me and said, "I know what you mean. How can I help you?"

I stopped milking and turned looked up at him as I said, "You know I got this music thing in me and I'm worried that I can never be the musician I should be because I don't read music. And I'm just getting started down that path, but what do,..." I lost my train of mind and paused.

My dad waved bits of debris off a bench seat, that looked like it was an ancient part of the barn, and he sat down. I kept milking, looking down in the milk bucket, not wanting any interaction with my dad after I was so

dumb in what I was trying to say.

My dad looked over at me and waited for me to give him eye contact, and after I could no longer ignore what I knew he wanted, I stopped milking and when I looked over into my dad's eyes; his face seemingly shining from the 120-watt hanging lightbulb. His face turned to concern as he said, "What I've learned here in this life is you gotta do the best you can with the gifts that you've been given." Then my dad stands up, still looking down and says, "You gonna be done with that pretty soon. I gotta go to work."

Back to "**But The Music**," If you listen to this song from its heartfelt perspective you may find what it was that I was trying to accomplish when I wrote this piece. There are times when I sit down at the piano and play chords and I feel the music; it does something to my very soul that I could never describe. I have never reveled in my magic fingers or my wonderful dexterity because I've never really had such magical fingers or great dexterity. But

sometimes I get touched deeply and it can be a combination of chord progressions or a tune that I sing while I accompany myself either on the piano or guitar or it might just be the feeling floating around, to be a part of a journey, and the small parts and voices join each other to create a new creation. There's no way I can ever say what the whole music thing gives me, or for me to be able to give back to all of you, and yes, whatever it is, it's real and it's in me.

The lyrics to this song just seemed to float out as I sang the song. Also, the circus-like polka music driving this song is remarkable. And here we have accordion music, hmmm. But seriously what instrument better to polka with? Church-like organ slows down and accordions play,... and all is still,... for a moment and then the circus is back in town.

Centuries ago, poets and musicians accredited these wonderful things to the muses or special gods of creativity to the arts. From some present-day spiritual perspectives, we would call them distinct abilities or gifts or talents. I'm truly thankful that I have been given the opportunity to identify and hopefully magnify the special gifts given to me by God. And as the song says in the chorus,

"But the music, the music is my life,
and maybe in my time I may yet see it shine.
All the music, the music is my way
to end a turmoil day and cast my cares away."

I may yet see it shine but it gives me great satisfaction to hear my children singing my songs and the thought that perhaps my songs may be listened to long after I have passed away brings me a sense of fulfilled peace and an inner joy that perhaps my music and song will continue on,...

Side Note:

Over the years I have wondered what it is like for Diane to be married to a hopeless dreamer,... a man that spends all his extra time writing poetry, composing accompanying music and then, recording songs or writing books,... meanwhile I'm thinking that it has to be a challenge for her to live with someone that is so sure that someday his creativity will be discovered,... , and after hundreds of songs, (a lot of them written for Diane),... most of the time she still maintains a pos-itive support,... after all, Diane could easily have said, "hey, wake up." and, "You're chasing an illusive dream, that's gonna let you down,..." and for years Diane has felt the pains that I have carried, the pains of never being validated, and secretly knowing that the real reason might be that I am, *'Just Not Good Enough'* or that the times have changed and Lord Baldwin's material is not what anyone wants anymore,

Meanwhile, Diane continues to support me in all my endeavors anyway,... and as I continue to believe in what I'm doing, I gotta love that woman even that much more because I know,... Diane doesn't have to believe in my dream to believe in me,... and I know with a warm assurance that in spite of my shortcomings, *'She Loves Me Anyway'*

98

20 - PLASTIC ON PLASTIC

- 1993

99

NOTES ABOUT THE COVERS

Notes On The New Cover:

This cover was more to my liking. This picture depicts plastic containers of all sizes, manufacturers and brands. These pop bottles (and other plastic bottles), are being compressed into a large cube. (more about that later in the notes).

I know little about this process but I am confused why there's so many tops or lids still on the bottles. I've been told from our recycling people that the two different plastics are not compatible and the lids need to be thrown away. Still, this picture was close to what I wanted.

Notes On The Original Covers:

So, truck with rocks or garbage truck dumping garbage in a landfill? Arguably neither was a good representation of our worldwide plight and how we deal with plastic and recycling,... challenges escalate where the chemicals used in the production of plastic are toxic and a detrimental to the human body,... so many bad chemicals are in plastic,... like lead, cadmium and mercury which can directly come in contact with us human beings as well as animals in the wild and all of our ocean creatures. These toxins can cause cancers, congenital disabilities, immune system problems and childhood development issues.

PLASTIC ON PLASTIC

Plastic On Plastic
What Happened To The Rest?
What It Was All About
The Runner
I Couldn't Help From Crying
So Hard To Be Heard
I'm Too Tired

101

Plastic On Plastic

Plastic on plastic, for storage and show,
So much left over with nowhere to go.
Containers storing hot, containers storing cold,
containers that survive past the products they hold.
In the ceilings, on the counters, in the floors the walls,
plastic on plastic is surrounding us all.

Plastic on plastic, for its purpose, succeeds,
transcending out beyond the consumer's wants and needs.
Old beer cans, aluminum, dead cars on the street,
can all be melted down with a little bit of heat.
But piled up in heaps, then, vastly melted down,
plastic on plastic will still be around.

Plastic on plastic, with questionable worth,
sitting on roadways and cluttering the earth,
Scattered in homes, strewn long and tall,
clogging up the landfills and choking us all.
And if we can't control it and put it in place,
plastic on plastic will survive the human race.

Plastic on plastic, will be here to stay,
as mindless individuals think they can throw it away.
"Recycle," Some say, is solution that's fair,
but few get involved, and the rest just don't care.
Here we wait too long till we're in way too deep,
while plastic on plastic is a monster asleep.

102

What Happened To The Rest?

What happened to the rest?
The just rewards that come with even quiet victories.
Prestige and recognition, saved up then for the best.
What happened to the rest?
What happened to the rest?
So many were in favor of this cause we felt was right.
They rallied around the ethics; our standards carried high.
And when we won, our struggle seemed unjustified or less;
but what happened to the rest?
The feeling of relief with that foe out on the run.
The Quiet peace in knowing that the evil was undone.
There was a sickness in the triumph as we could not contest,
oh, what happened to the rest?
What happened to the rest?
The confidence within the vanquishing of all the wrong;
his crimes exposed, his exile, freedom ruling strong,
and afterwards, oh how our cause would crest.
Oh, but where are they? Where is the restoration?
I'm waiting here to join them for that final celebration;
oh, what happened to the rest?

103

What It Was All About

When I was young, our gang was best,
around the neighborhood scene,
with Brothers more, and Brothers less,
while I fit in between.
No challengers could hope to beat
the Brother's Family Crew
and together we all ruled that street
and everybody knew.

It was all for one and one for all
like young boys could be men.
A quiet strength, a stronger wall, protected us back then.
Although lives change and thoughts might turn,
as they travel different routes,
that family bond, the real concern,
was what it was all about.
That was what it was all about.

Little dreams die, and big dreams wait
as life goes on with talk.

The roads lead out; obscure and great,
as we chose the path we walk.
We have our families all in place
to try to make dreams last,
and when I see them cooperate,
it reminds me of that past,

where it was all for one and one for all
like young boys could be men.
A quiet strength and a stronger wall
protected us back then.
Although lives changed and thoughts might turn,
as I travel different routes,
oh the family bond, that real concern,
was what it was all about.
Hey, that was what it was all about.

104

The Runner

He's a chemist, and working in a mobile lab;
he's brewing up the batch that will finally pay his tab.
He's a husband, but his work comes out on top,
and he knows where she lives if he should ever stop.

He's a runner, running from his wife;
Up and down the West Coast, higher than a kite.
He's a runner, running for his life.
Running out of daylight, running in the night.

He's a farmer, growing plants under bright lights,
and he's harvesting the crops when the marketplace is right.
He's a shyster, with a heart that's cold as ice,
and he finagles every deal to get the better price.

He's a runner; he's running with a knife.
Up and down the West Coast, running out of sight.
He's a runner, running for his life.
Running into problems and running in the night.

He's a business man, willing to take the dare;
knows how to move his products, anytime, anywhere.
He's a, banker; he turns a profit now and then.
Yeah, he's a gypsy, always on the move again.

He's a runner; he's running from the light.
Up and down the West Coast, running left and right.
He's a runner, he's running for his life.
running out of options, and running in the night.
Oh, he's running into problems
and running in the night.

I Couldn't Help From Crying

I couldn't help from crying, when I found that you were on the run.
I never stopped from trying to find out what I'd done.
I couldn't sleep at all last night,
didn't know who was wrong or right,
but I couldn't help from crying,
when I found that you were gone.
I couldn't help from crying, when I found that you were gone.
I never stopped from trying, babe,
to find out what train or bus you got on.
I couldn't help but wonder,
saw no rain heard no thunder,
where I made my big blunder
to make you pack your bags and go.
I couldn't help from crying, when I knew that I was on my own.
I felt my heart was dying, sitting in the house alone.
I couldn't sleep at all last night,
and didn't know who was wrong or right,
but I couldn't help from crying,
when I found that you were gone.

106

So Hard To Be Heard

It's all so obvious to you, and it's all right there in view,
still it seems so sad not to carry it all through.
You'd like to say "Let me tell you what's going on."
But when the courage finally comes, the moment is gone.

Oh, why do we take so long to say the words.
Oh, why do we make it so hard to be heard.

There's so much happening with the kids, the house is never done;
jamming on priorities, you're always on the run.
You'd like to know that sometime, there is purpose in your life,
and maybe have some listening ear to appreciate his wife.

Oh, why do we take so long to say the words.
Oh, why do we make it so hard to be heard.

I keep thinking, "It'll wait." and, "The right time will come."
I try not to think anymore about what's being done.
So, I just put it all off, thinking maybe it can wait.
I never do communicate or try to set things straight.

Oh, why do we take so long to say the words.
Oh, why do we make it so hard to be heard.

With so much happening with this job, I'm hardly ever home.
When I finally do have some time, I just want to be alone.
Thinking you don't really care to hear about my life,
I never share those little things that otherwise I might.

Oh, why do we take so long to say the words.
Oh, why do we make it so hard to be heard.

107

I'm Too Tired

I have practiced and worked throughout my youth.
Studied all the great masters; emulating all they do.
Now I finally reached a creation for myself,
I've perfecting quite a style, nothing like anyone else.
As my colors mixed to sing a different call,
all my brushes tell the story of the canvas capturing all.
Yet with all the time spent with loving care,
I stand on this street corner with no buyers for my wares.

I'm too tired to go on.
I feel like my life has all but come and gone.
And I'd like to give in, sure I'd like to give up,
with the way that I feel because I've just had enough,
of the agencies and shops, the managers and hoods,
who promise quick results but never do deliver goods;
as they display in the hallways and or never at all;
talent sitting in dark closets or stacked up in the halls.
I know within my heart if a chance would come my way,
I could make it to the top and paint my life away.
But I'm too tired to go on anymore today.

I have worked as hard as any man unteached,
I have paid this bitter price
to achieve these goals I've reached.
And it's sad a select few control this mass;
if they don't like your work,
well you might as well pump gas.
So I wait for my chance to finally shine,
working on my masterpiece, to be ready for the time.
Thoughts of self-worth, self-esteem confuse my head,
and I realize my statements are hiding and left unsaid.

I'm too tired to go on,
and I feel like my life has all but come and gone.
I'd like to give in, oh, I'd like to give up,
with the way that I feel, I've just had enough,
of those crowds on the sidewalk
s, seeking Dali to match their rugs.
Saying to me, "With all this talent,
it's hard to pick the right one."
They admire, and they compliment;
they flatter words of praise,
but when it's time to lay their money down,
they sander off, away.
and I'm too tired to go on anymore today.

108

Let Me Know Why

It's a sad game that we have to play,
when nobody knows the right words to say.
So, we take it in stride, it's all part of life,
but we never resolve all these problems inside.

It's always the same, we never relate,
and we secretly feel it's the other to blame.
But we need to erase the doubt
and work these things out.

Let me know why, you're feeling so mad, or sad;
What's bothering you down inside, let me know why.
Hey, let me know why, we're drifting apart, you start
to tell me but then you just hide, hey, Hon,
let me know why.

It's a sad end to write off a friend,
as nobody wants to give in or bend.
Let it go day to day, hoping it'll go away,
while love and understanding is all it would take.

Still, this anger remains through a cause of charades
while our love in the balance and it's slipping away;
we need to come back in the light
to make these things right.

Let me know why,
we're not getting along, what's wrong?
We can't do much more till we try,
oh, let me know why. Let me know why,
I'm on the wrong track, to get back
if you want everything back in line,
let me know why.

109

MEMOIRS & NOTES - 20 - 'PLASTIC ON PLASTIC'

Plastic on Plastic

(1993) I guess it's essential to note as I begin my tirade on plastic, and it's important to keep in mind that plastic itself is a unique material with many benefits: it's cheap, versatile, lightweight, and in many forms, plastic has resistant qualities.

This makes it a valuable material for many functions. It can also provide environmental benefits: it plays a critical role in maintaining food quality, safety and reducing food waste. The trade-offs between plastics and substitutes (or complete bans) are thus complex and

Sea of Plastic Bottles

could create negative impacts on the environment without it.

The year. 1993. Plastic pollution was having a negative impact on our oceans and wildlife health. We were generating huge amounts of plastic waste worldwide, but the United States led the way. The management of plastic waste that would determine the risk of plastic entering the ocean was almost nonexistent and the mismanagement of waste was going unnoticed, even though President Clinton and Vice President Gore had come into office committed to demonstrate that a clean environment should be their goal. But the United States would ship off their plastic waste to other middle- and low-income countries that had poor or nonexistent waste management policies, and thus, a lot of our plastic ended up in the oceans, creating the main sources of global ocean plastic pollution.

The Clinton-Gore Administration was working to have a cleaner environment than the previous administration by tougher enforcement of environmental laws, strengthening public health standards, and protecting irreplaceable national treasures, with hopes of giving our nation the cleanest air and water in generations, but, with an estimated 40 percent of all plastic waste in the oceans coming from the United States, clearly there was a problem.

I went out to the dump one day and I saw semi-trucks completely filled with crushed plastic gallon milk containers, pressed and bound with baling wire into large cubes. I asked a man what was to happen with all those plastic milk cartons asking where they were going. He told me that there are places that recycle these types of milk cartons, but at the time, those facilities had too much plastic already and for the time, were not taking any more. And then, because the recyclers had no takers for their plastic, the cubes were in holding patterns at the dump. He was half joking around when he said that, if all the plastic was to be melted down, there would still be a big blob of plastic, and if you melted that big blob of plastic down, you would still have a big blob of plastic.

After that, I realized how much we all rely on this thing called plastic. But there was also the realization that we have a problem disposing of the plastic itself after we are done with it. And I don't want to sound like an alarmist because I know a lot of plastic can be recycled and there's a lot of good that comes from recycled products, but sometimes, we create things with plastics without any concern for its own lifecycle or recycle abilities, and we find ourselves watching the black smoke rise from fires burning down the unwanted plastics, but unfortunately, not away.

What Happened to the Rest?

(1987) There was a break-in that occurred on the night of June 17, 1972, and five burglars entered the Democratic National Committee offices at the Watergate office complex in Washington. As they became implicated, several of President Nixon's top aides eventually resigned after the U.S. Senate began televised hearings, investigating the conduct of the White House officials. During these Senate investigations, it was revealed that the president had bugged the oval office and recorded sensitive conversations on tapes.

Ten days after Spiro Agnew resigned, on the evening of Saturday, October 20, 1973, during the Watergate scandal,

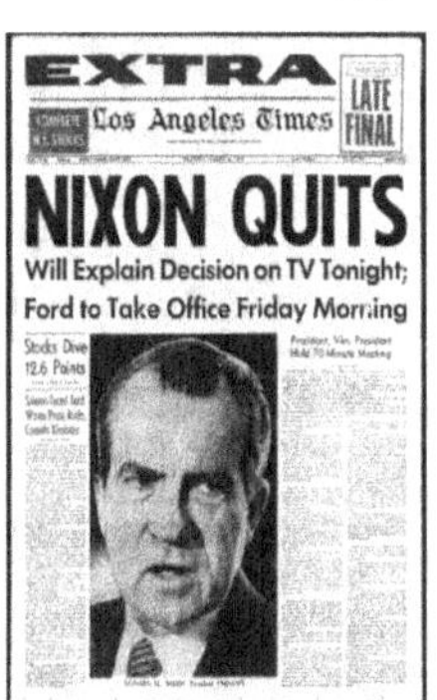

Nixon ordered his Attorney General Elliot Richardson to fire Special Prosecutor Archibald Cox to slow down or squelch the process. Richardson refused and resigned effective immediately. Nixon then ordered Deputy Attorney General William Ruckelshaus to fire Cox; Ruckelshaus refused, and also resigned.

Nixon then ordered the third-most-senior official at the Justice Department, Solicitor General Robert Bork, to fire Cox, and Bork kowtowed and carried out the dismissal.

The House Judiciary Committee also began to question whether President Nixon and his actions might have committed impeachable offenses. Although before this, the Republican Nixon administration attempted to cover-up its involvement; during the hearings that followed, the scope of the scandal became apparent and the existence of the Nixon White House tapes was revealed.

In the spring of 1974 Nixon, feeling the pressure, and wanting to minimalize his possible role in the illegal break in, released certain edited transcripts of 42 taped White House conversations relevant to the Watergate cover-up and were finally made public; showing Nixon for the cynical, paranoid individual he was.

After a two-year battle against government agencies, a loss of support from the Congress, the Senate, the House of Representatives, as well as the U.S. Supreme Court, who, without dividing into their usual, partisan lines, put their biased differences aside, to take the health of the nation as its priority, and was supported even by the news media. President Nixon began to break down.

On August 8, 1974, President Richard M. Nixon spoke on TV to the American public and announced his decision to resign the presidency of United States. Of course, Nixon's decision came after the Judiciary Committee of the House of Representatives voted to recommend his impeachment, and we, the pawns and victims of the Vietnam War era, wanted retribution and reconciliation for all his heinous crimes. On that day, Friday, August 9, 1974, I still remember leaning my head out the two-story window of the Chinese Castle apartment off Hawthorn Blvd. in Portland Oregon that we were living in at the time. And screaming a loud, victorious hail to the god of impartiality, validity and rightfulness, I felt that justice had been served. And I was not alone. There were hundreds of other people doing the same, yelling out their windows, or honking their car horns; everyone everywhere was celebrating the resignation. Later the next day, I gathered with many of my friends and we toasted the new day and the ousting of the evil dictator.

Although the Vietnam War was not over yet, our struggle and resistance seemed to have made a difference and we were all in great exhilaration as we talked of the new days to follow. I also reflected on some of the lyrics from the Jefferson Airplane's song, "Volunteers of America" had possibly and prophetically come true. And yet another turn of events happened, that twisted our best laid plans, as Vice-President Gerald Ford, who succeeded Nixon, granted Nixon a full pardon for any crimes he might have committed while being president. Although it was a time to heal, a time for us as a broken America to move forward, like many other Americans, I was left with a hollow sense of emptiness and injustice that has been carried by me as well as many others, even to this day. This sense of injustice, that hollow emptiness inside; these feelings are part of what I was trying to portray when I wrote the lyrics to this song. These feelings were not only made more poignant with the Ford administration, followed by the Carter administration, and then the ravishment and outrageous assault on the economy via the middle class of America by President Reagan.

Our new day, that wonderful enlightened new era never materialized. Instead, a good part of the baby boomer's generation left their hopes and dreams for that better America by selling out to the highest bidder. Unfortunately, money and power has always attracted, tempted, allured and seduced some of the best of us. There are some, like myself, still holding the torch of the true hippie movement, not willing to sell out, waiting in the wings, looking at each successive presidency with scrutiny hoping this time we won't get fooled again; continuing in our own way to work towards that restored world with a hope of that improved tomorrow.

Side Note:

this song was written in 1987 and recorded in 1993, less than a year before Richard Nixon passed away in 1994. By this time I was given a computer lab of my own to manage at SPSCC, which had a television placed up high by the ceiling in the front corner of the room. On that day that Nixon passed away, I was asked by some of the students to turn it on so they could watch the proceedings. And we watched as the news media hyped his death into something powerful, even moving, and I admit that I almost fell into the trappings of that event, but, curse my reactionary hippie heart, I remained distant and aloof, still remembering friends that never came back from Vietnam and remembering certain events and happenings of that bloated, mismanaged war that should have ended differently and should have ended many years before it finally did.

Another Side Note:

"*What Happened To The Rest?*" and what happened to my generation stepping up to make a better place for us all to live? What happened to learning from our mistakes? What happened to the rising generation with its people and leaders that would have a sense of honor, stand with uprightness, equitability and civil rights to people of colour and not be swayed by the devils that tempt and corrupt with money and power; what happened to that generation endowed with honesty that bear their honor in serving with integrity? What happened to not selling out to the man? And, what happened to the rest?

What It Was All About

(1991) This song is about the life and times of a kid with the camaraderie he had with his family. Although a lot of my early life has been painted as an unhappy time with a restrictive childhood with an unsympathetic, domineering and uncaring stepfather, I know now that it was because of my adversity and my need to lean on my brothers and later in my teens,  even my sisters, that I grew up with a strong support of love.

My mother did her best to shelter and protect me from myself and against the evils of the world as well as or especially, Senior, but it was my relationship with my older brothers, John and David, and my brother Richie that I remember so vividly and made me feel like we were all a part of a great supportive organization and I knew that I would always be sheltered and protected by them. We have a name for that now, and it's called family, but back then we didn't call it that, we called it a gang, and it was our gang.

The Runner

(1992) This song chronicles the life and times of two different people, their struggles to find themselves in the world that they had created for themselves, situated in a dangerous environment that they both walked into everyday. One of the two people is still alive, I believe, but I haven't seen him for too many years. It still amazes me that someone can walk that tight rope of danger in the streets, juggling a life of illegal drugs, dealing with unstable and highly dangerous individuals while all the while skirting a risk of being picked up by police and being thrown in jail or killed by the competition, or some addict or some petty thief or pickpocket in the street; maybe good money, but what a dangerous, unpredictable life. Still, I wish him well.

Side Note:

The last time I saw Louie he was in 1974 when he moving from his place on Southwest Columbia Street in Portland to somewhere in Southeast Portland with the help of another friend, Sylvester. By this time, Louie had a lot of plants and we transported them in Sylvester's VW van. It was a scary time for me to even be involved in the move and I kept trying to think of an excuse if and when we were pulled over by the police, and I was so relieved to finally get the plants moved into Louie's new place where he had a second-floor balcony of veranda that he used as his greenhouse and then get the heck out of there. As I was leaving, I looked up and could see Louie's plants kind of hanging over the rails, plants that were unmistakably marijuana, and thought to myself, If I know what those plants are, surly an observant policeman would,... but to my understanding, Louie never got busted.

I Couldn't Help From Crying

(1971) This one goes way back and is another one of my first guitar songs. It made me feel extra good to do this one. Its conception happened one day as I was walking from Louie's place to my own. I pulled out my harmonica and created that little riff that comes at the end of each stanza. The phrase, "I couldn't help from crying" just popped out about three blocks from my Kingston apartment in Portland, and upon arriving, I sat on the bed, strummed out the chords, wrote down the words, all in about 20 minutes.

For some time, this was a favorite of Richie and Ray's and we would play it over and over and over. And Richie was getting good at playing the harmonica part too.

One day I was jamming with the boys and started playing this tune but with little to no interest from the other guys, it seemed drab and unexciting to me, like it just lost its magic and so, I never played it again. It was kind of like that time when I was going to Portland State University and I had eaten too many peanut butter and jelly sandwiches; you know what happens, you just get to a point where you've had enough and you move on to tuna fish sandwiches. I really did find an old friend when it came time to record this tune and I was happy to be able to capture the essence of the harmonica music as well as what this song was to me and will continue to be.

So Hard To Be Heard

(1991) Like so many other songs in the past, present and probably will continue in the future, I think too much to try to philosophically put down on paper incidents and feelings that might have had at a particular moment of influence, or clarity, or disaster, or retrospect. But it is really true that in an argument, or just to make a point sometimes, our anger blinds us into believing that silence will heal the circumstances and then when it is time to work things out, we seem to only have loud voices and very bad hearing. I am as guilty of this as anyone, but I find myself amazed sometimes that I can be so stupid and that I can justify things with the most ridiculous logic. But life is never a done deal till we make it so, and although there is no time to waste, I seem to find plenty of excuses not to be timely. The communication between two people that care for each other is just do dang important. (Dang? I don't think I've ever used that adjective before). But seriously, life is too short for enmities between couples that love each other.

I'm Too Tired

(1981) I have a good friend named Terry who is very talented in art, as a painter of landscape pictures and portraits. With oils and acrylics, Terry has an eye for putting things together in just the right way that makes the difference between simple art and a brilliant masterpiece. Still, after seeing much of his work sitting around, drawing dust, unable to create a market for, and him feeling frustrated to the whole process, and maybe knowing that after he'd be done creating his works of art that he couldn't make money on, he'd still have to do for his and his family. So, one day, Terry stopped painting pictures and portraits and took a different direction in his life and went into a field that was kind of art related, and he is doing well. Yet Terry's magic and creativity; that special eye and steady hand for detail, was all put away as he chose to stop painting and create no more.

Perhaps there is a strong parallel between the music industry and painting for the fine arts, but I know there was no easy road to success without commitment beyond what compromises most are willing to undertake, and yes, I did draw that correlation between this painting individual and my own frustration with the music business. I was always trying to get noticed; letters to record companies, going to Bars at night looking for positive reactions and maybe the right person to help me be discovered, playing on radio stations on an afternoon in the middle of the week, hoping to be heard by someone out there going to open mike performances, knowing that the only ears hearing my material are those of other musicians, many of which are sizing me up and comparing my stuff with theirs, while preparing themselves to sound as good or better than the act that they were just listening to. There were many times that I got so sick and tired of hearing people say, "why don't you do something with that music?" Oh my goodness; it got to the point where it was hard to realize it was their way of complementing me, and that they were not saying why are you so lazy. But they could never know the struggle I experienced trying to promote myself, the disappointment and frustration I would go through having radio stations refuse to play my tapes or the costs and hassles I dealt with sending letters to record companies and people that I was told were part of the business only to get negative, (if any) responses to my requests. (Diane found my collection of rejected letters from those many record companies buried in the bottom of my dresser years ago and threw them away). But this ongoing frustration that I had felt for so many years is now not so burning, not so important; now, it matter less because I'm not working towards that illusive commercial gain as much anymore. I am my biggest fan and because I do it for myself, I can't wait to do another song, compile, engineer and master a new album, and for me, for now, being able to draw from that continual well of creativity is enough.

Let Me Know Why

(1985) I know there is no easy road to success without a commitment to open communication from both sides and a willingness to go beyond what most people are willing to go. I think that the road to reconciliation in a relationship begins with a realization from both sides is that perhaps my own poor communication skills are more to blame than the negative action that triggered the problem in the first place.

And sometimes we think the other knows what is going on in our head and heart so we choose to be silent, but many times, if we could just let the other person know what we're thinking, or why we're doing what it is that we're doing, it might start the process of breaking down the barriers we've made. And letting go or sharing information about those pent-up feelings, we may even solve some of the underlying problems that have helped escalate things to some unhealthy degree.

Spring Winds Of Appommox

(1992) – I should apologize and be sorry for the fact that this title should have been, "*Spring Winds of Appomattox*," not Appommox but I'm not unhappy, even though it does kind of screw with the intent of the piece. I've already told the spell check in MS Word that it's the correct spelling of a word and it's too much trouble to reverse the spell check and is recognized in my album that's already been published and distributed and is already being streamed worldwide.

After the fall of Richmond, the Confederate capital of the South in the Civil War, on April 2, 1865, all of the officials in the Confederate government, including President Jefferson Davis, quickly fled. The dominoes began to fall.

The Battle of Appomattox Court House, (a township place in Virginia, not a building or courthouse), fought in Appomattox County, Virginia, on the morning of April 9, 1865, was one of the last battles of the American Civil War (1861–1865). It was the final engagement of Confederate General in Chief, Robert E. Lee, and his Army of Northern Virginia before it surrendered to the Union Army of the Potomac under the Commanding General of the United States, Ulysses S. Grant.

Appomattox Court House, was historically significant for its association with the Confederate General Robert E. Lee's surrender to the Union's Lieutenant General, Ulysses S. Grant on April 9, 1865.

Appomattox Court House - April 09, 1865

My inspiration to writing this instrumental piece was me thinking about the mindset of General Robert E. Lee and what a devastating experience this must have been for him to have to go through the process of surrendering his 28,000 troops as well at the whole south, and right after just losing a battle that same day. But also, to have to represent the defeated army, after fighting so many battles, and over the course of four years losing so many fellow soldiers, (over 258,000 soldiers not to mention, maybe 30,000 civilians) and here he ends up, at the McLean family's home in Appomattox Court House. How terribly humiliating it must have been for him to have to humble himself while representing the eleven southern states.

Characteristically, Grant arrived in his muddy field uniform while Lee had turned out in full dress attire, complete with sash and sword. Lee asked for the terms, and Grant hurriedly wrote them out. All officers and men were to be pardoned, and they would be sent home with their private property—most important, the horses, which could be used for a late spring planting. Officers would keep their side arms, and Lee's starving men would be given Union rations. In my mind I thought of me being General Lee and stepping out of that building, looking out at the world, with everything changed, and praying to God that I'd made the right decision.

110

SOME AUTHOR'S NOTES

Lord Baldwin; Playwright, Songwriter, Keyboardist, Guitarist, Songer/Performer and Jazz Harmonica Player. Emerging from the 60s rock era, has developed a distinctive and rather eclectic style that blends blues, jazz, folk and rock.

In 1983, Lord Baldwin had a renaissance and revitalization to his songwriting and performing and from a renewed perspective and sense of value, after reevaluating priorities, realizing the blessings and strengths of his family and friends, his own special style began to surface; through his poetry and music he documented his life and times.

As new songs began to flow, (even from within his dreams), Lord Baldwin documented the words, (poetry-lyrics), while they were fresh in his mind and he mentally documented the music that would eventually accompany the lyrics.

In 1989 or was it 1990, Lord Baldwin purchased a 4-track, Tascam Cassette Recorder, and immediately began to record. He then took the songs and engineered them into albums, each 45 minutes, so as to fill each side of a 90-minute cassette.

From that simple beginning, Lord Baldwin continued his analog recordings for the next ten years (1991 to 2001), into what has come to be known as, **"The Archive Series"** which is comprised of thirty-eight albums as well as six experimentation instrumentals and other compositions. This here is the **Second Book** of Lord Baldwin's anthological works, *'From The Lost Letters Sent;'*

'From The Lost Letters Sent – Book TWO: 1992 – 1993
Memoirs From An Invisible Songwriter'

Documenting the lyrics and memoirs of songs, musical compositions and stories from his **Second Nine albums:**

10 – **Heaven**
11 - **A Long Way From My Home**
12 – **You've Got To Believe**
13 – **A Family Man**
14 – **Another One Of Those Days**
17 – **Voices From The Past**
18 – **More Of The Same**
19 – **Expecting Rain**
20 – **Plastic On Plastic**

and documenting the **Sixty-Nine** poems to songs that were recorded between July of 1992 and May of 1993, where Lord Baldwin plays guitars, keyboards, pianos, harmonicas and all the other instruments as well as supplying all the voices to the recordings.

For the curious follower of Lord Baldwin music, this book can be also used as a companion while they examine an album, (presently streaming worldwide), they can also gain insightful stories that may accompany the songs they are listening to, and be able to read the lyrics as well as.

Lord Baldwin's heart-felt thanks go out to you for your interest and he wishes you well as you embark on this epic new journey.

III

INDEX BY NAME OF SONG

Index by Name of Song

Other Books
BY
LORD CHESTER L. BALDWIN II

FROM THE LOST LETTERS SENT
Memoirs Of An Invisible Songwriter
Book ONE: 1985 – 1992

FROM THE LOST LETTERS SENT
Memoirs Of An Invisible Songwriter
Book TWO: 1992 – 1993

FROM THE LOST LETTERS SENT
Memoirs Of An Invisible Songwriter
Book THREE: 1993 – 1994

FROM THE LOST LETTERS SENT
Memoirs Of An Invisible Songwriter
Book FOUR: 1995 – 2001

STEPPING BETWEEN THE ANTS
Book ONE: *The Winter Escape*

STEPPING BETWEEN THE ANTS
Book TWO: *The Spring Ahead*

STEPPING BETWEEN THE ANTS
Book THREE: *A Summer To Remember*

STEPPING BETWEEN THE ANTS
Book FOUR: *The Fall Behind*

RESILIENT:
A (Web-Based Episodic) Musical Play & Story

'HEADS' or,
'TALES FROM THE SUMMER OF LOVE'